STAR WARS®

CLONE WARS

ADVENTURES

VOLUME 7

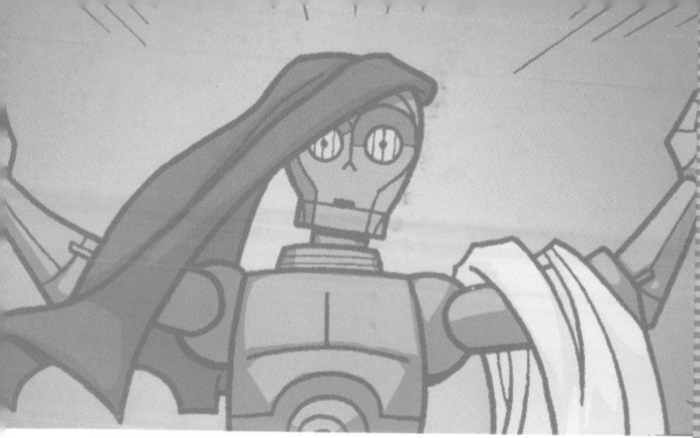

designers
Darin Fabrick and Josh Elliott

assistant editor
Dave Marshall

editor
Jeremy Barlow

publisher
Mike Richardson

special thanks to Sue Rostoni, Leland Chee,
and Amy Gary at Lucas Licensing

talk about this book online at: *www.darkhorse.com/community/boards*

The events in these stories take place sometime
during the Clone Wars.

Advertising Sales: (503) 652-8815 x370
Comic Shop Locator Service: (888) 266-4226
www.darkhorse.com
www.starwars.com

5 7 9 10 8 6 4

STAR WARS: CLONE WARS ADVENTURES Volume 7, January 2007. Published by Dark Horse Comics, Inc., 10956 SE Main Street, Milwaukie, OR 97222.

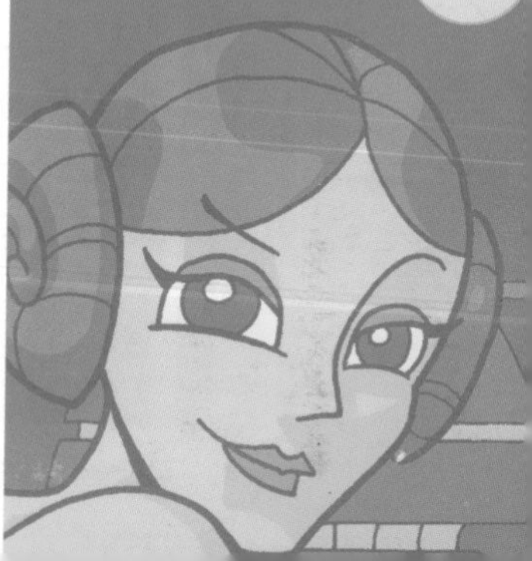

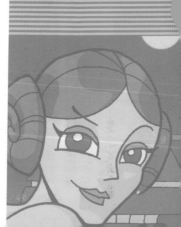

STAR WARS

CLONE WARS ADVENTURES

VOLUME 7

CREATURE COMFORTS
script and art The Fillbach Brothers
colors Ronda Pattison

SPY GIRLS
script Ryan Kaufman
art Stewart McKenny
colors Dan Jackson

IMPREGNABLE
script Chris Avellone
art Ethen Beavers
colors Dan Jackson

THIS PRECIOUS SHINING
script Jeremy Barlow
art The Fillbach Brothers
colors Ronda Pattison

lettering
Michael Heisler

cover
The Fillbach Brothers and Dan Jackson

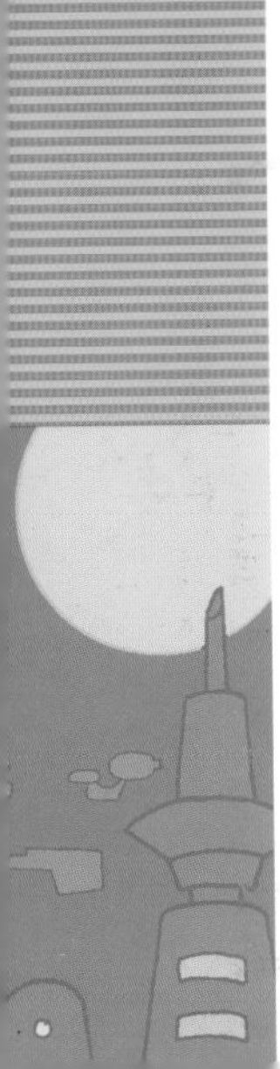

Dark Horse Books™

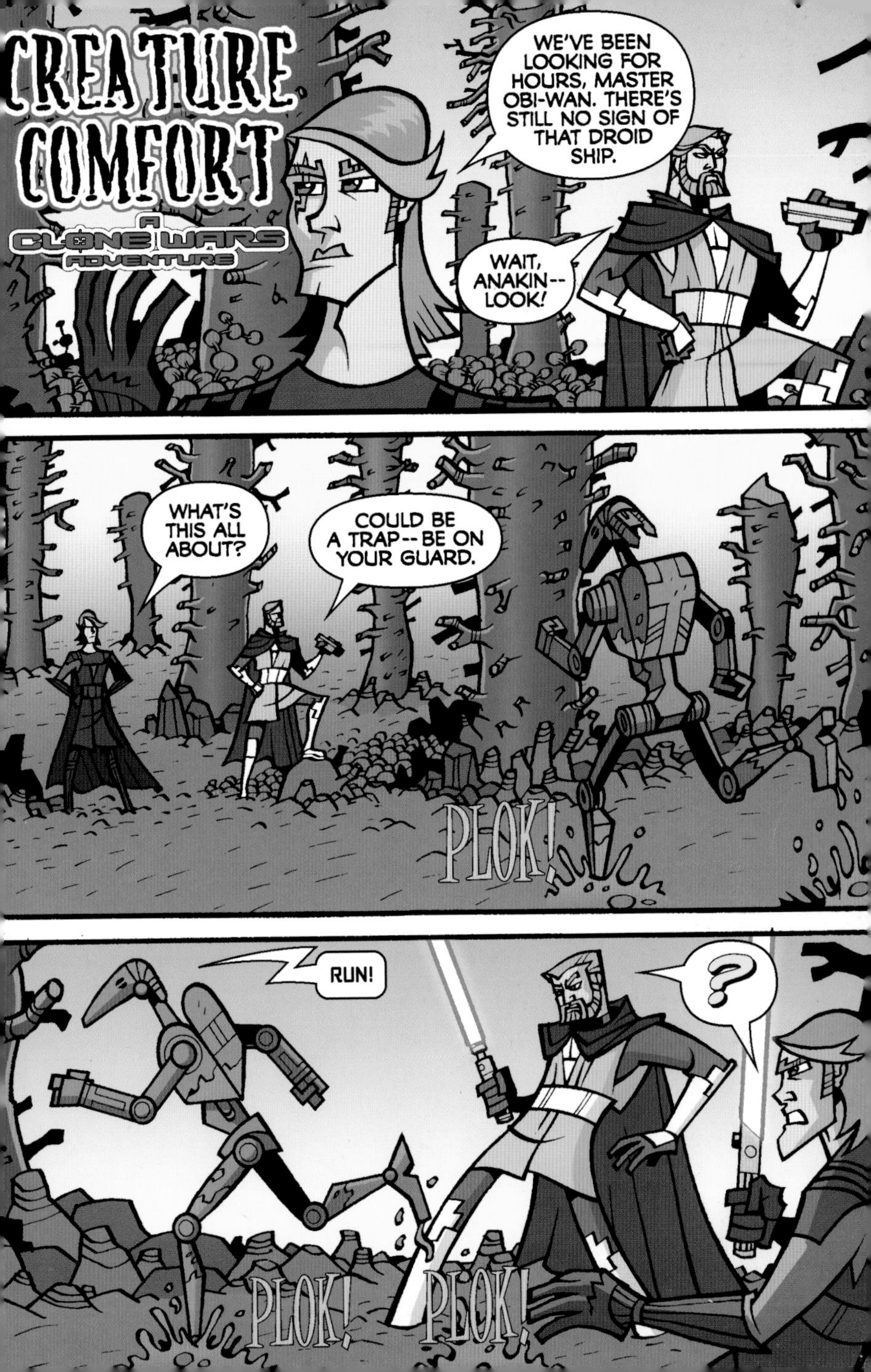
CREATURE COMFORT
A CLONE WARS ADVENTURE
WE'VE BEEN LOOKING FOR HOURS, MASTER OBI-WAN. THERE'S STILL NO SIGN OF THAT DROID SHIP.
WAIT, ANAKIN-- LOOK!
WHAT'S THIS ALL ABOUT?
COULD BE A TRAP--BE ON YOUR GUARD.
PLOK!
RUN!
?
PLOK! PLOK!

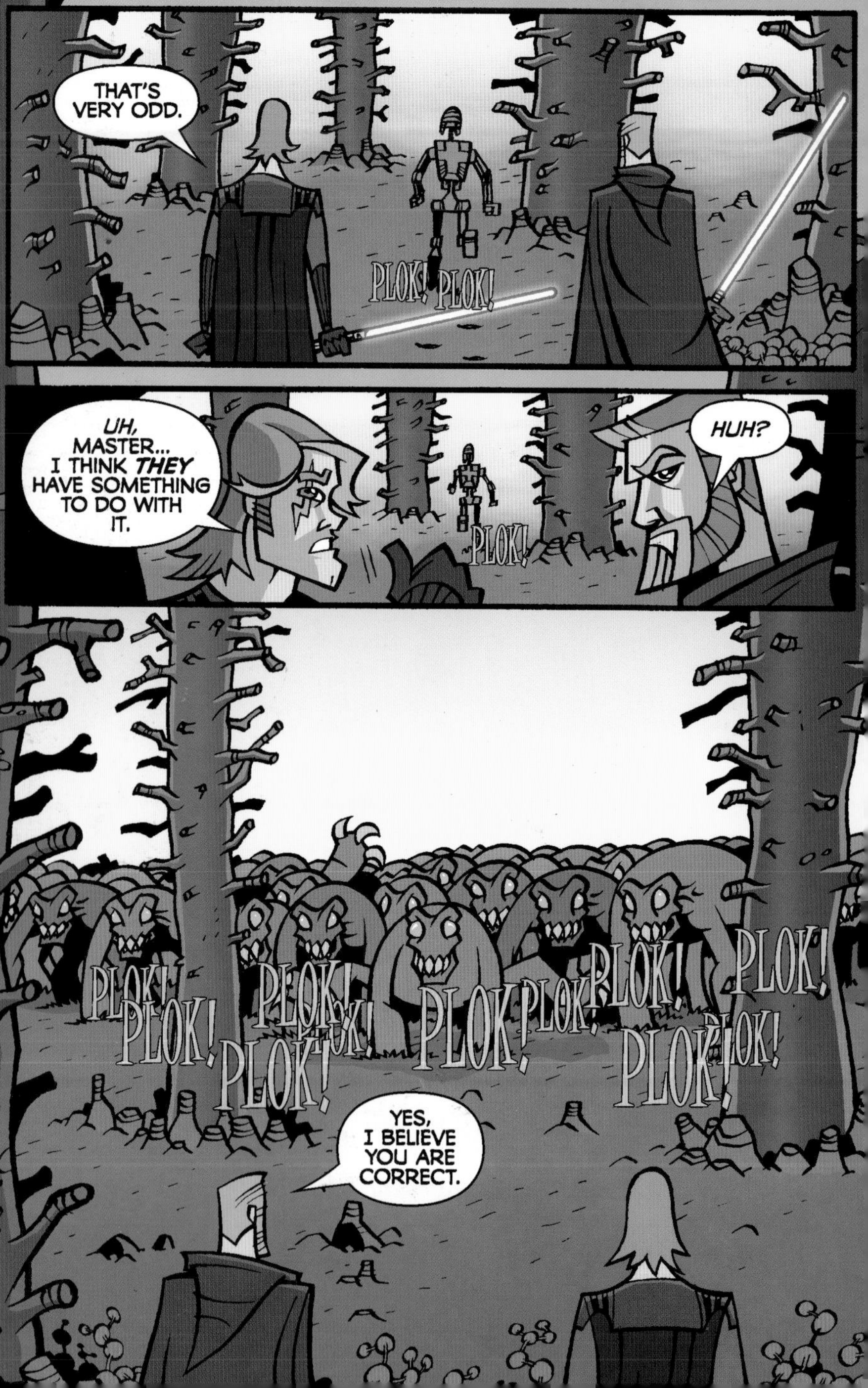
THAT'S VERY ODD.
PLOK! PLOK!
UH, MASTER... I THINK THEY HAVE SOMETHING TO DO WITH IT.
HUH?
PLOK!
PLOK! PLOK! PLOK! PLOK! PLOK! PLOK! PLOK! PLOK! PLOK! PLOK! PLOK!
YES, I BELIEVE YOU ARE CORRECT.

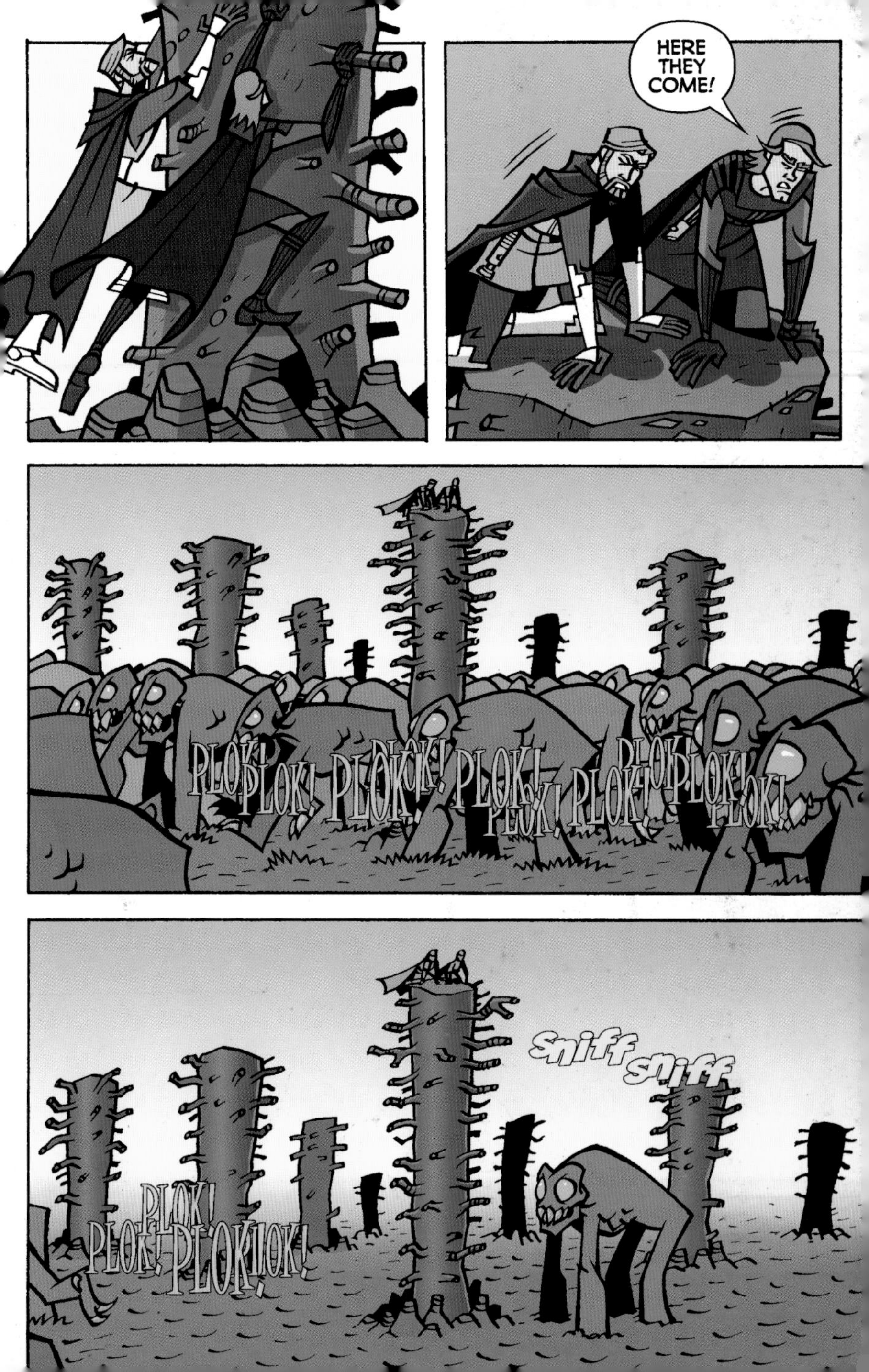
HERE THEY COME!
PLOK! PLOK! PLOK! PLOK! PLOK! PLOK! PLOK! PLOK! PLOK! PLOK! PLOK!
Sniff Sniff
PLOK! PLOK! PLOK! PLOK!

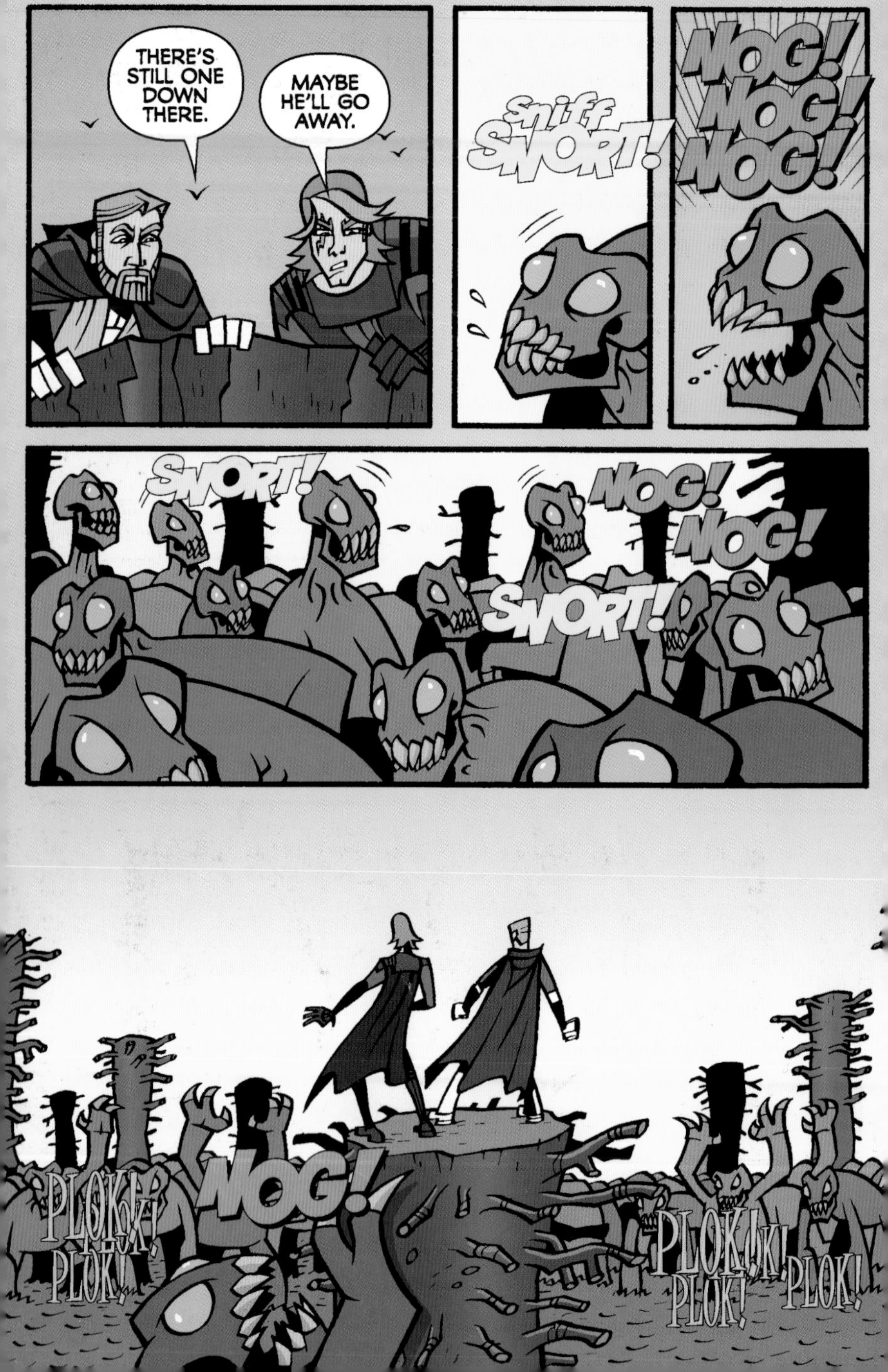
THERE'S STILL ONE DOWN THERE.
MAYBE HE'LL GO AWAY.
Sniff
SNORT!
NOG! NOG! NOG!
SNORT!
NOG!
NOG!
SNORT!
PLOK! PLOK!
NOG!
PLOK! PLOK!
PLOK!

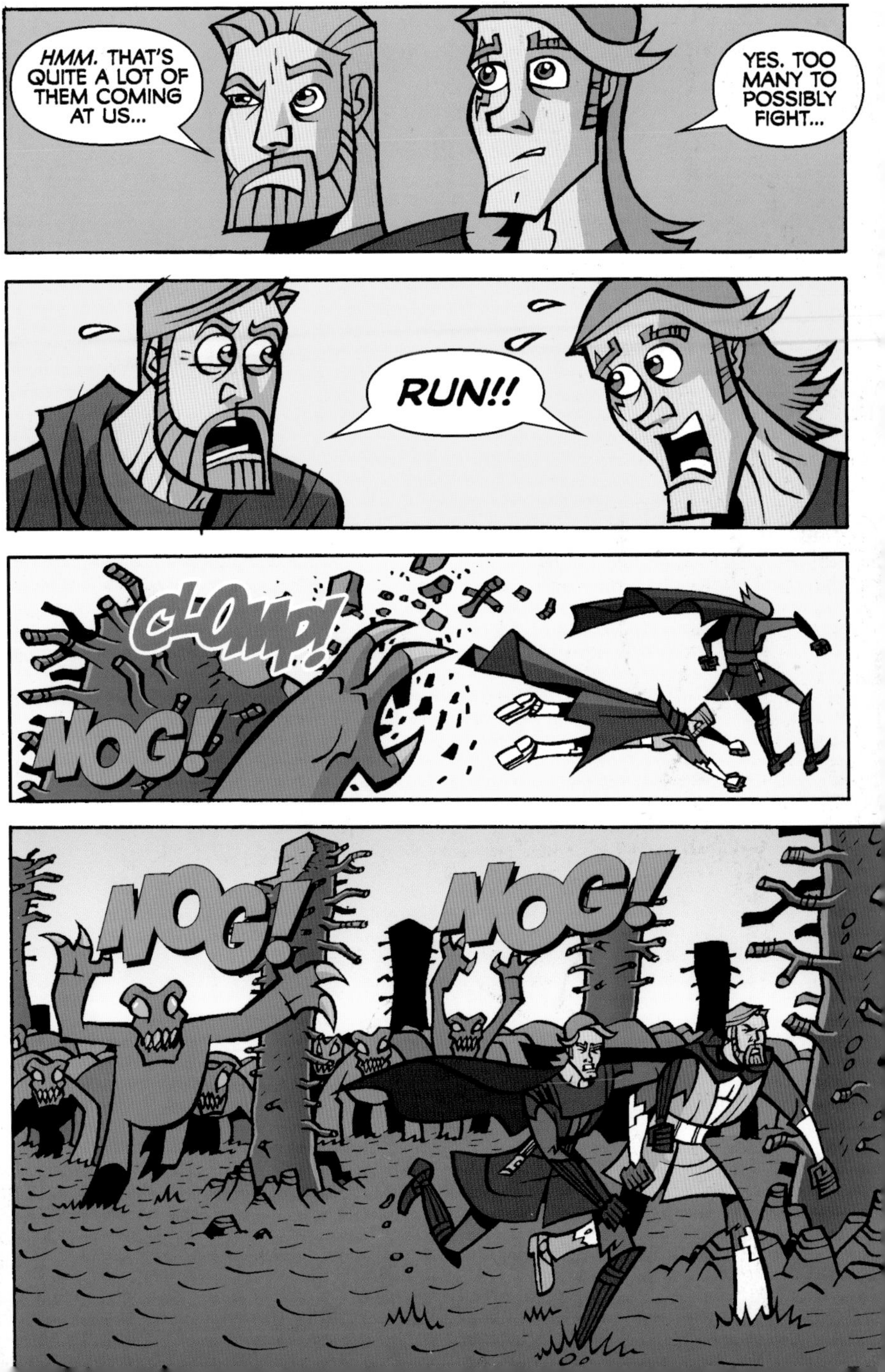
HMM. THAT'S QUITE A LOT OF THEM COMING AT US...
YES. TOO MANY TO POSSIBLY FIGHT...
RUN!!
CLOMP!
NOG!
NOG!
NOG!

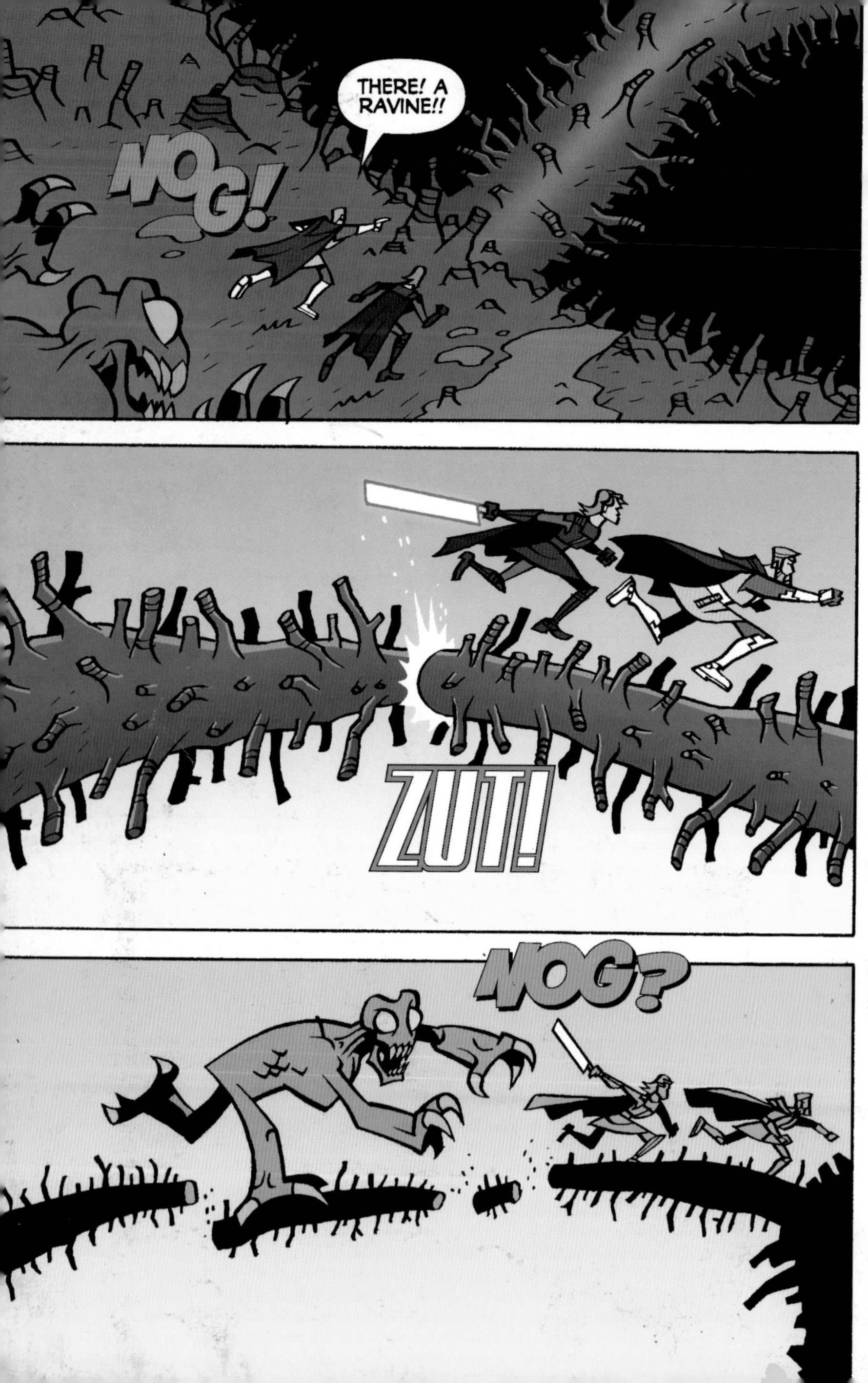
NOG!
THERE! A RAVINE!!
ZUT!
NOG?

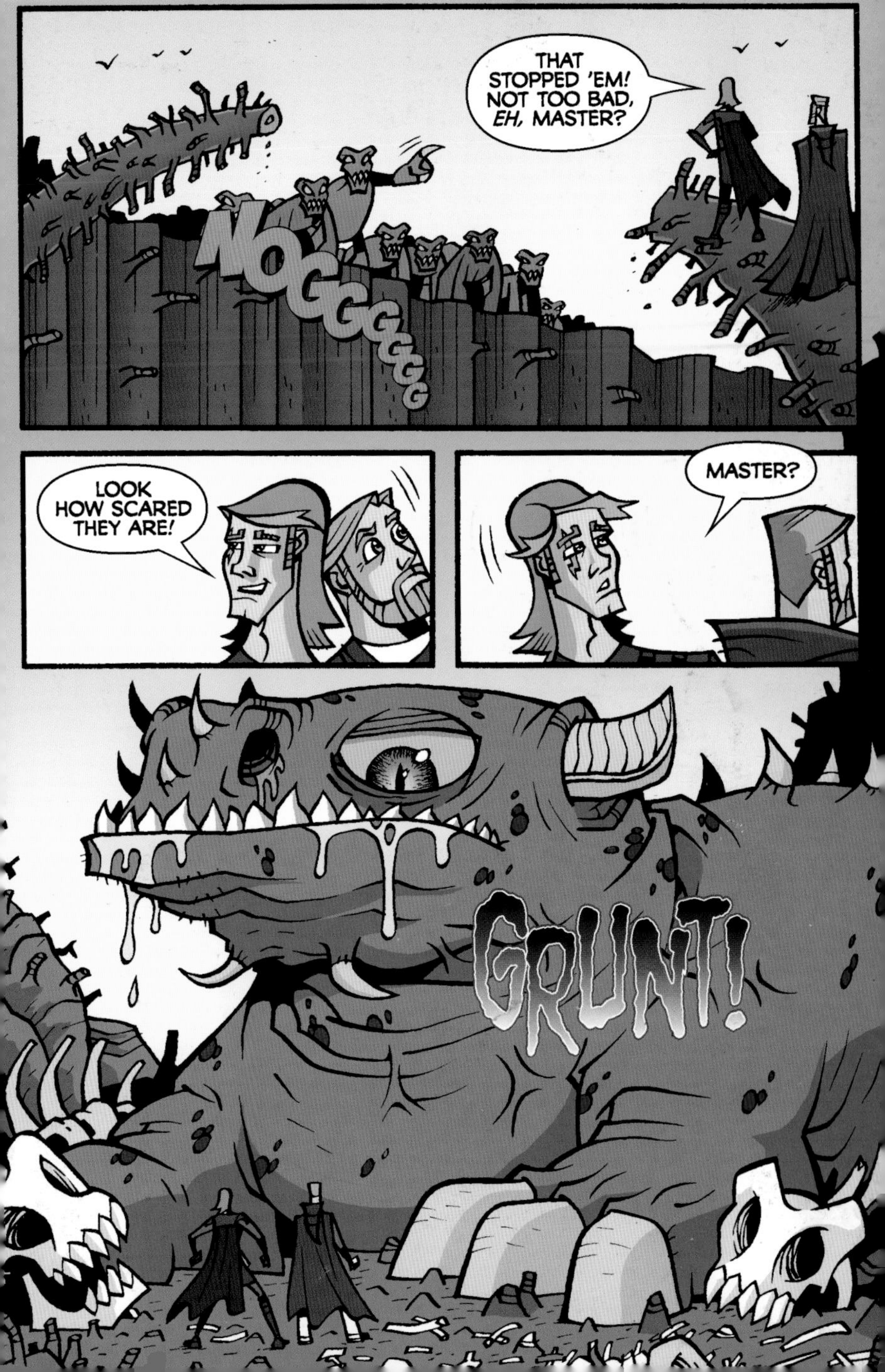
THAT STOPPED 'EM! NOT TOO BAD, *EH,* MASTER?
MOGGGGGG
LOOK HOW SCARED THEY ARE!
MASTER?
GRUNT!

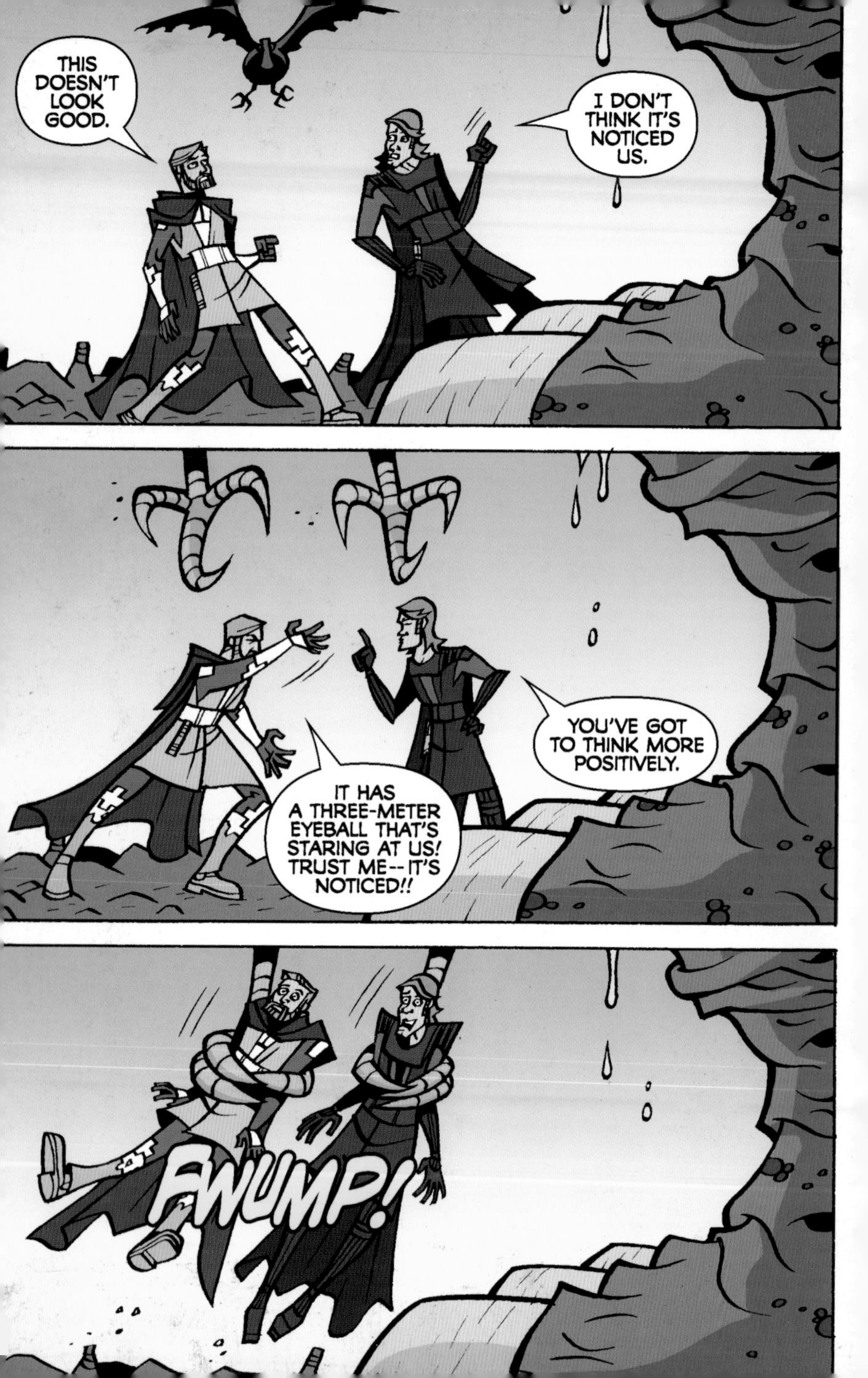
THIS DOESN'T LOOK GOOD.
I DON'T THINK IT'S NOTICED US.
YOU'VE GOT TO THINK MORE POSITIVELY.
IT HAS A THREE-METER EYEBALL THAT'S STARING AT US! TRUST ME--IT'S NOTICED!!
FWUMP!

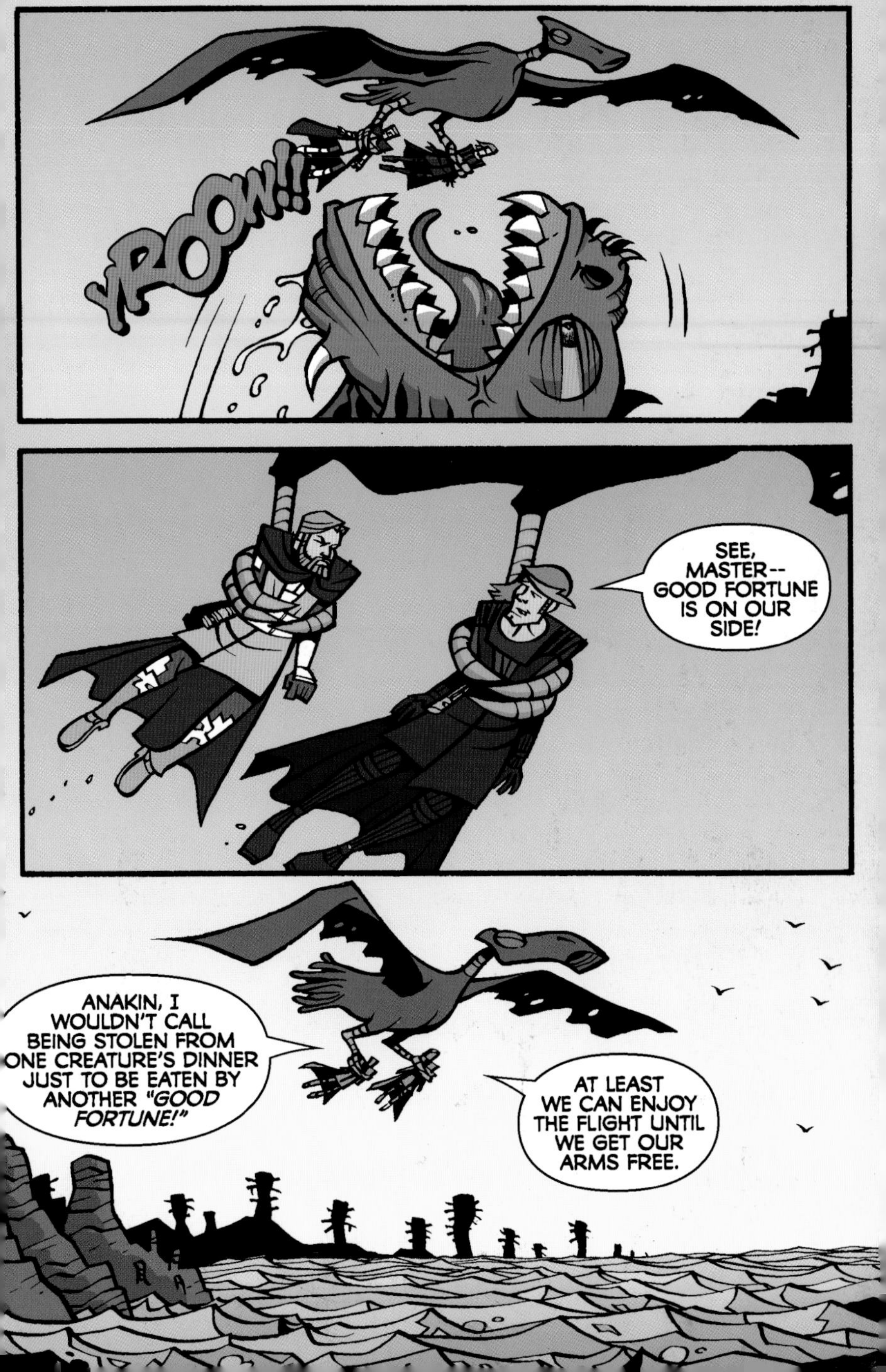
VROOM!!
SEE, MASTER-- GOOD FORTUNE IS ON OUR SIDE!
ANAKIN, I WOULDN'T CALL BEING STOLEN FROM ONE CREATURE'S DINNER JUST TO BE EATEN BY ANOTHER *"GOOD FORTUNE!"*
AT LEAST WE CAN ENJOY THE FLIGHT UNTIL WE GET OUR ARMS FREE.

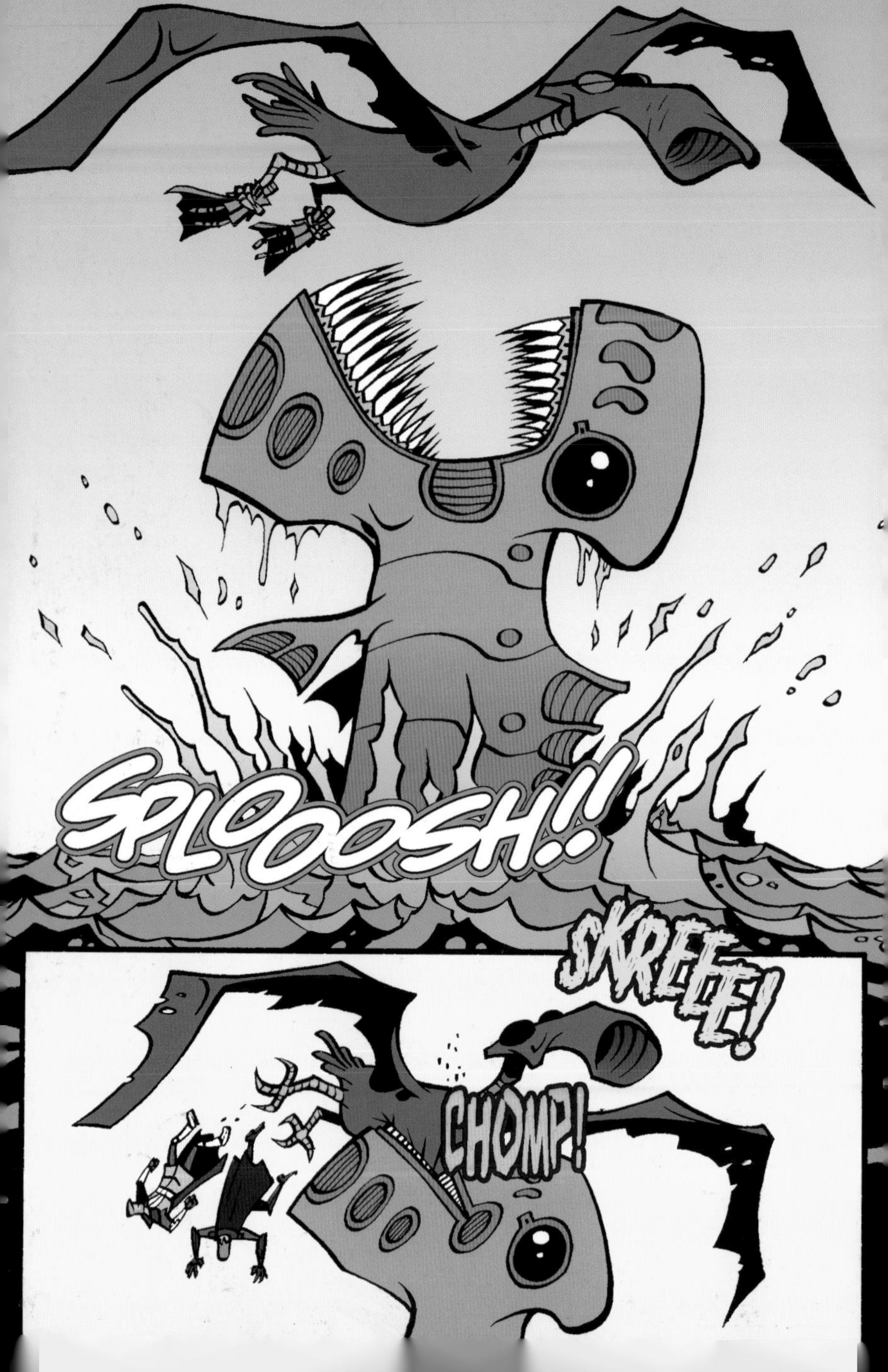
SPLOOOSH!!
SKREEE!
CHOMP!

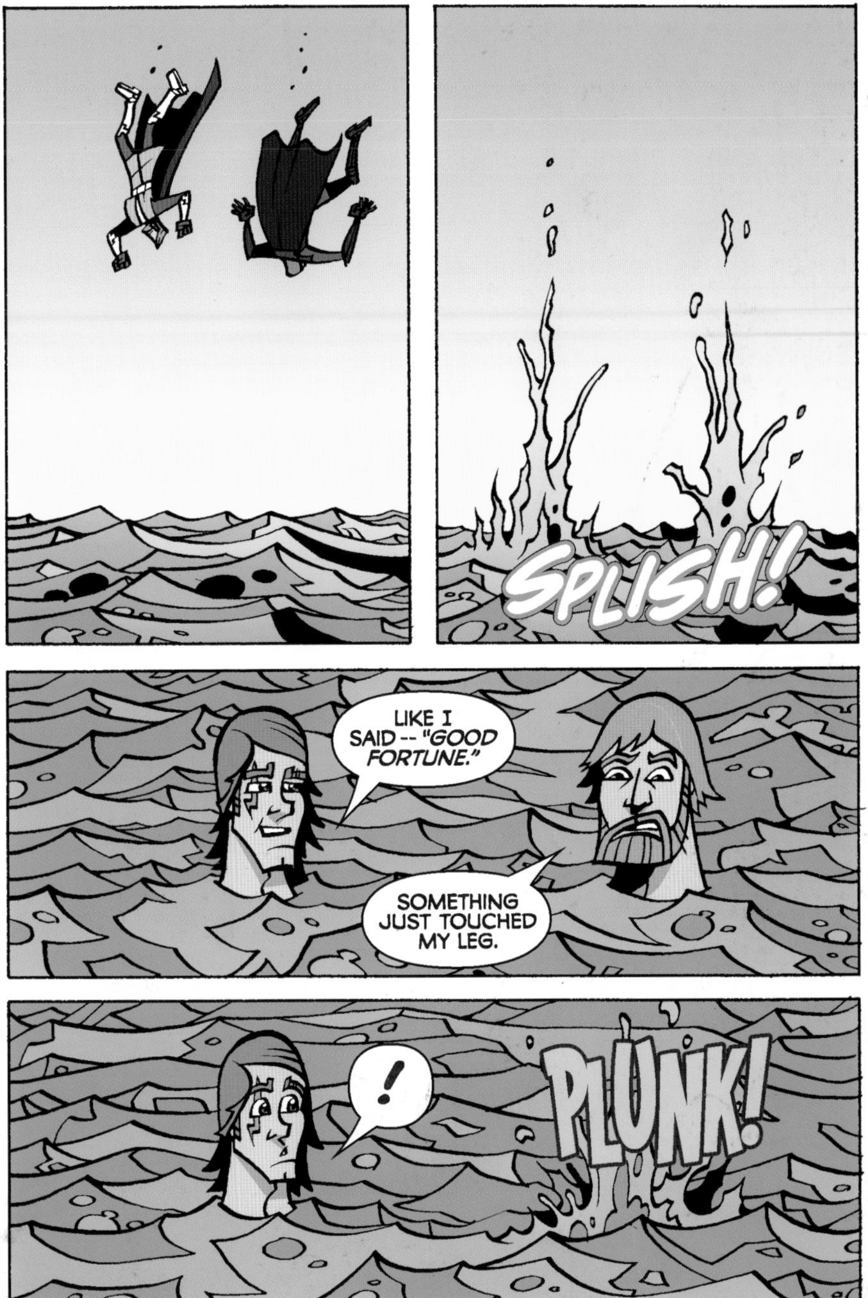
SPLISH!
LIKE I SAID -- "GOOD FORTUNE."
SOMETHING JUST TOUCHED MY LEG.
!
PLUNK!

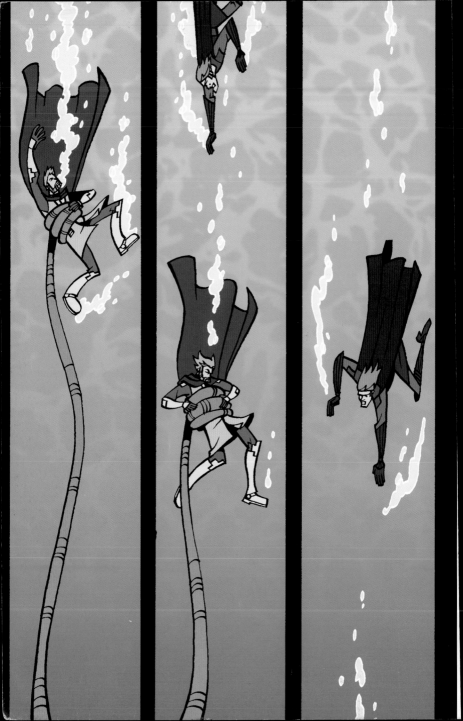

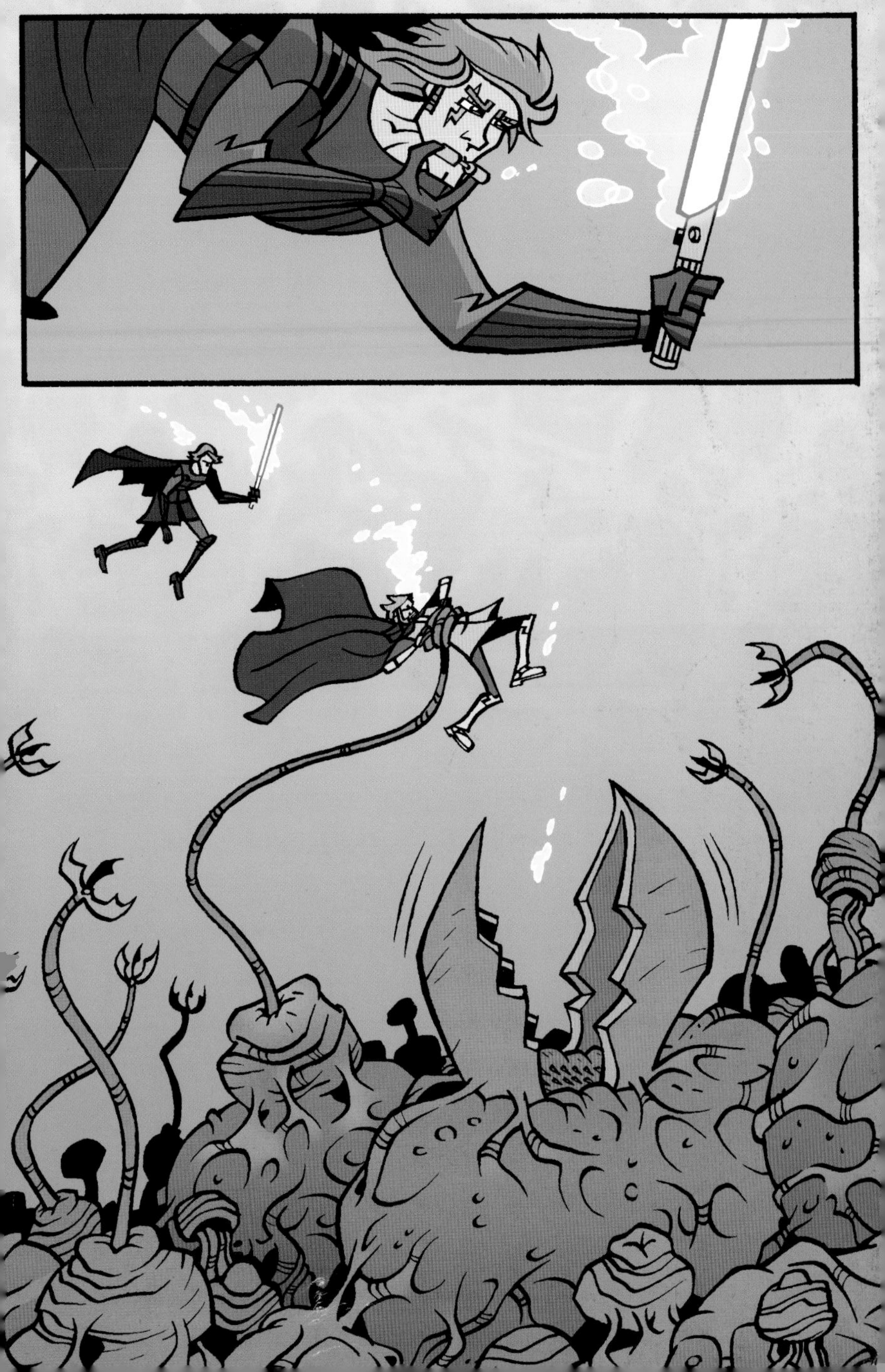

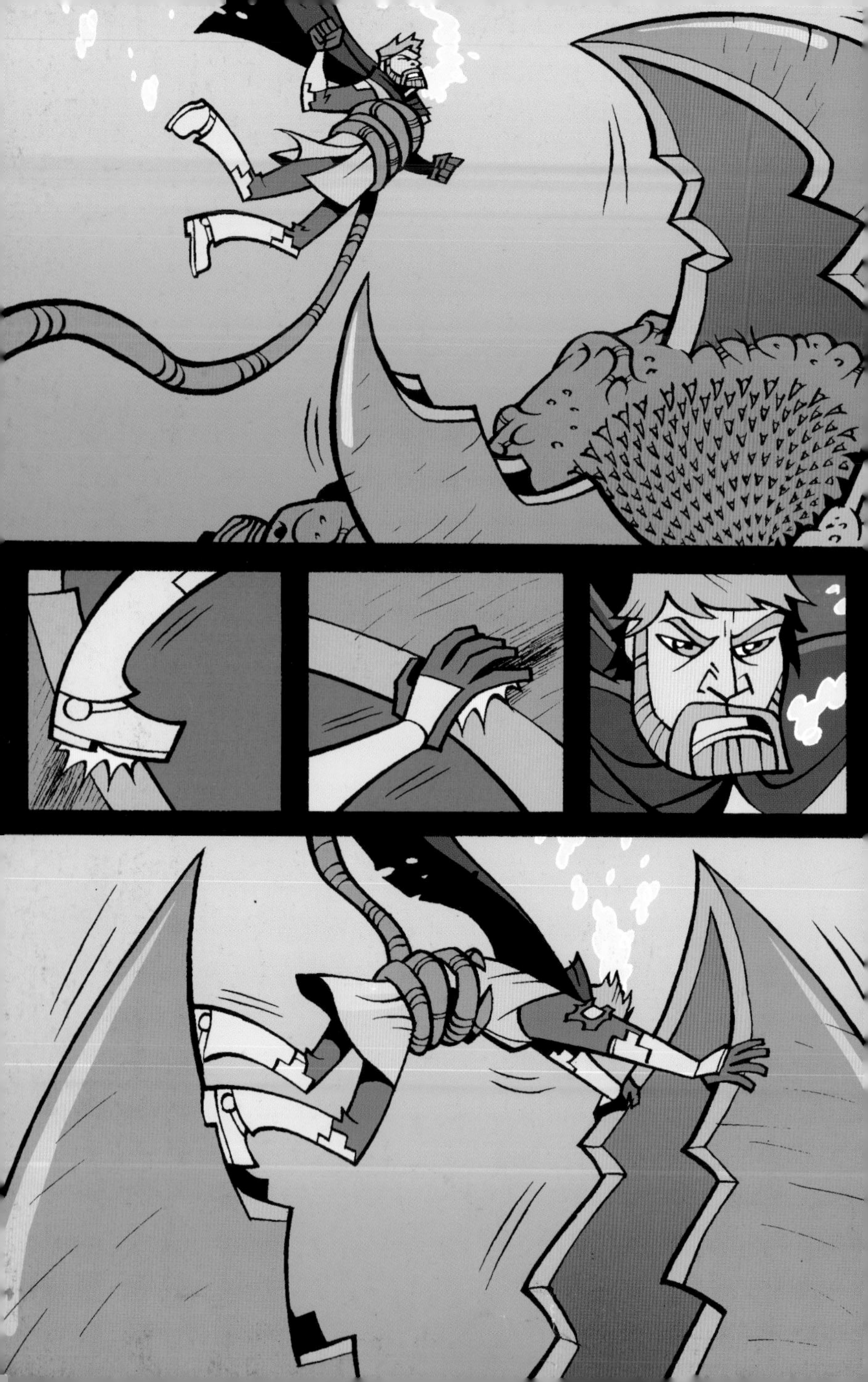

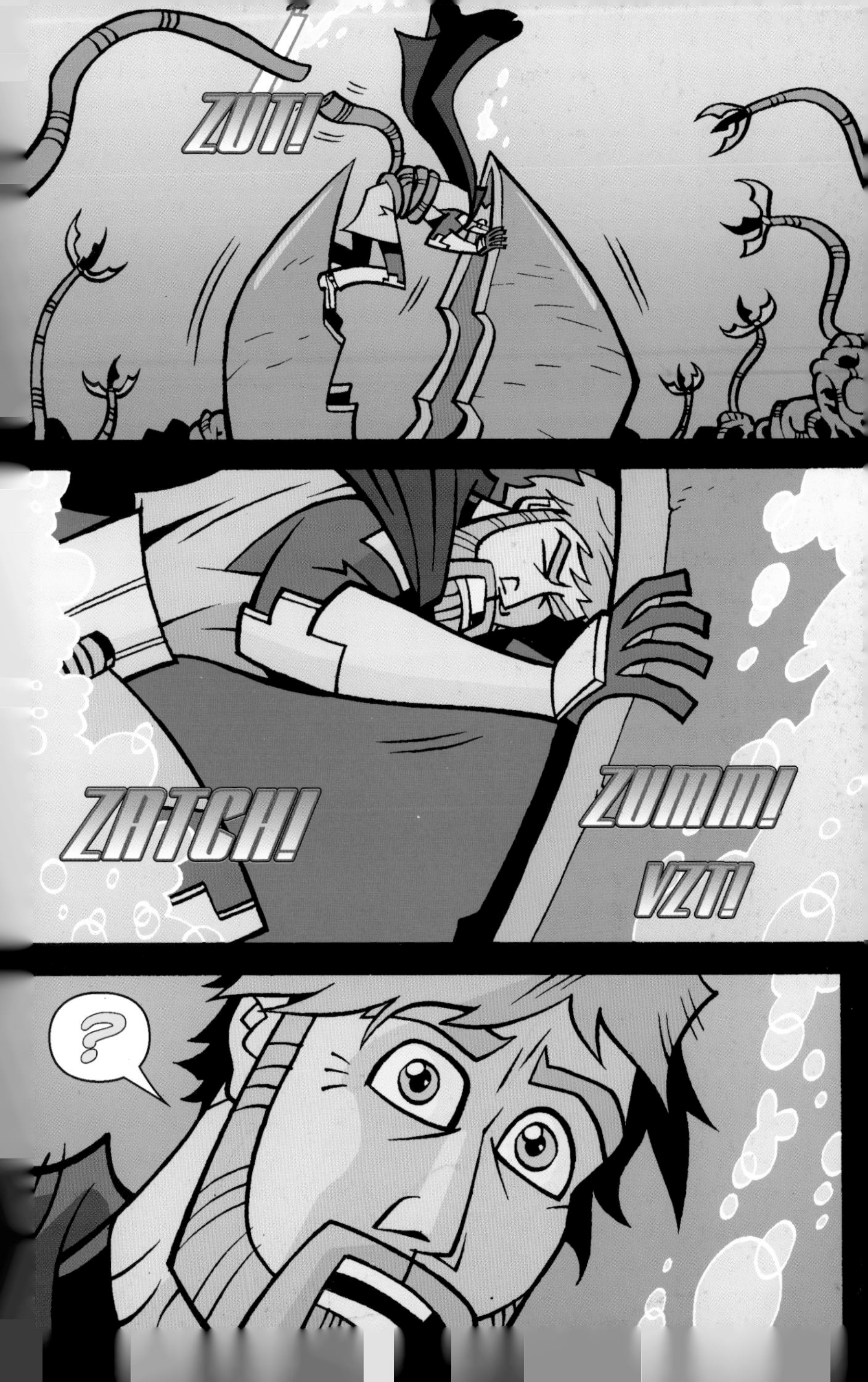
ZUT!
ZATCH!
ZUMM!
VZT!
?

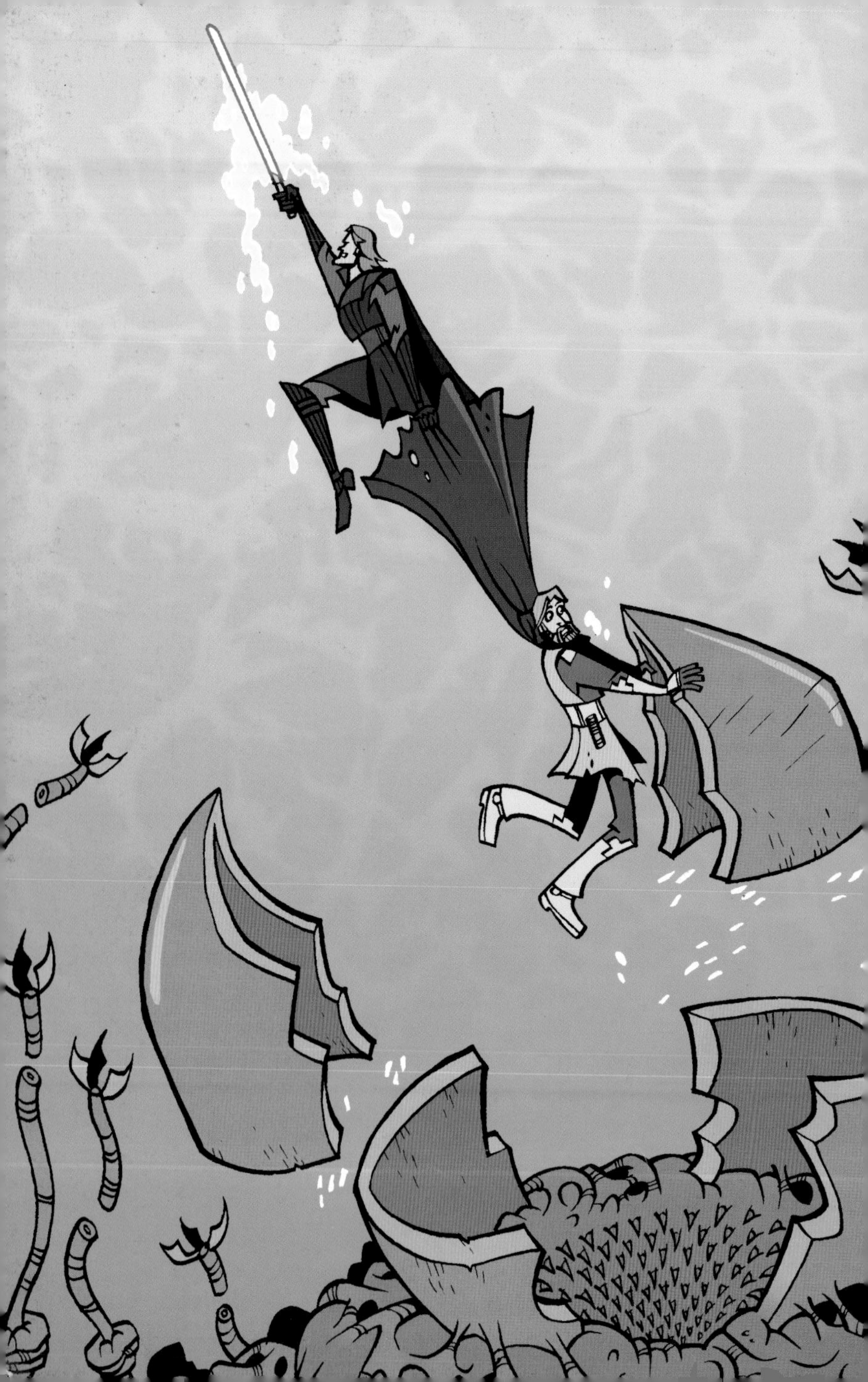

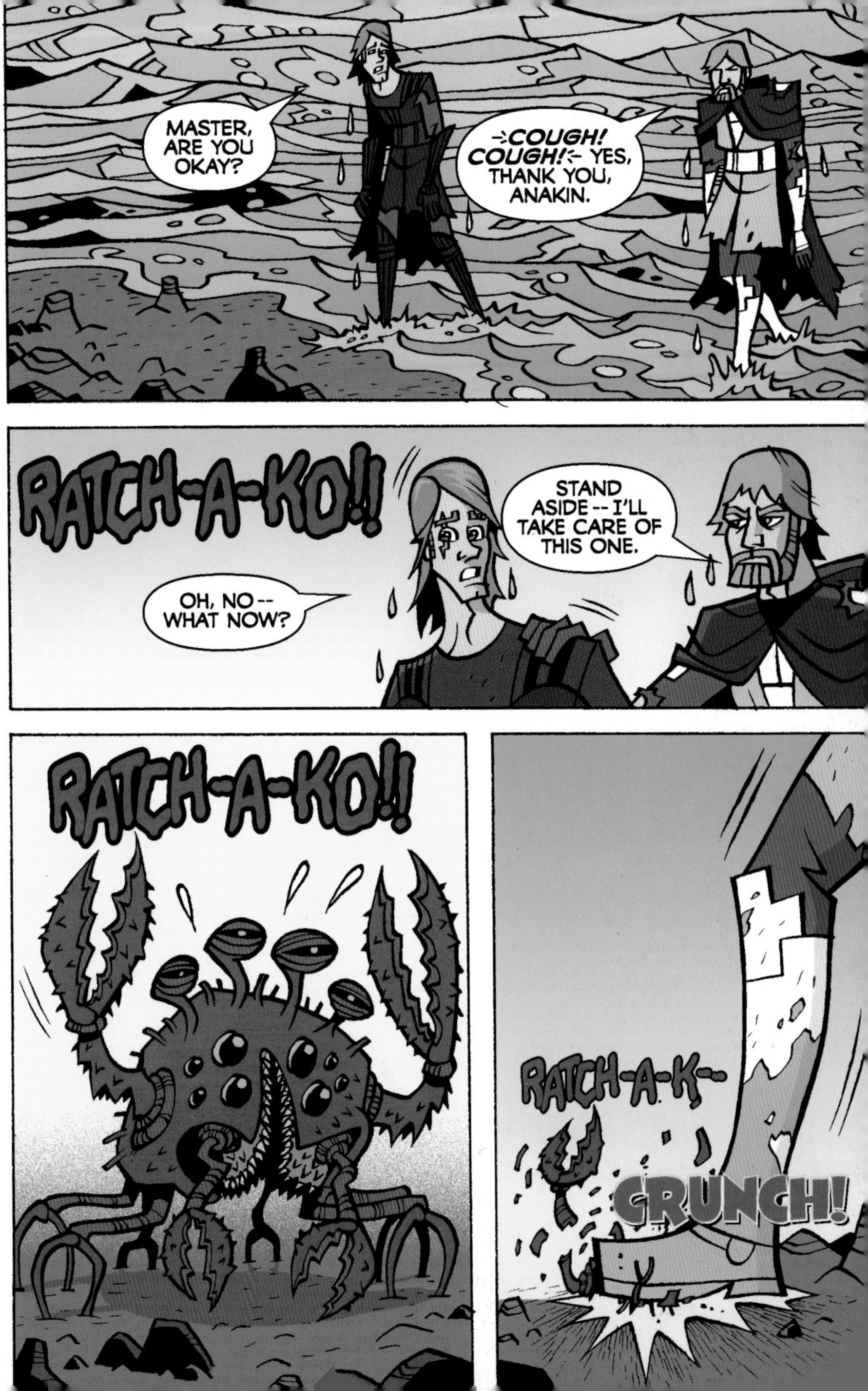
MASTER, ARE YOU OKAY?
-COUGH! COUGH!- YES, THANK YOU, ANAKIN.
RATCH-A-KO!!
OH, NO-- WHAT NOW?
STAND ASIDE -- I'LL TAKE CARE OF THIS ONE.
RATCH-A-KO!!
RATCH-A-K--
CRUNCH!

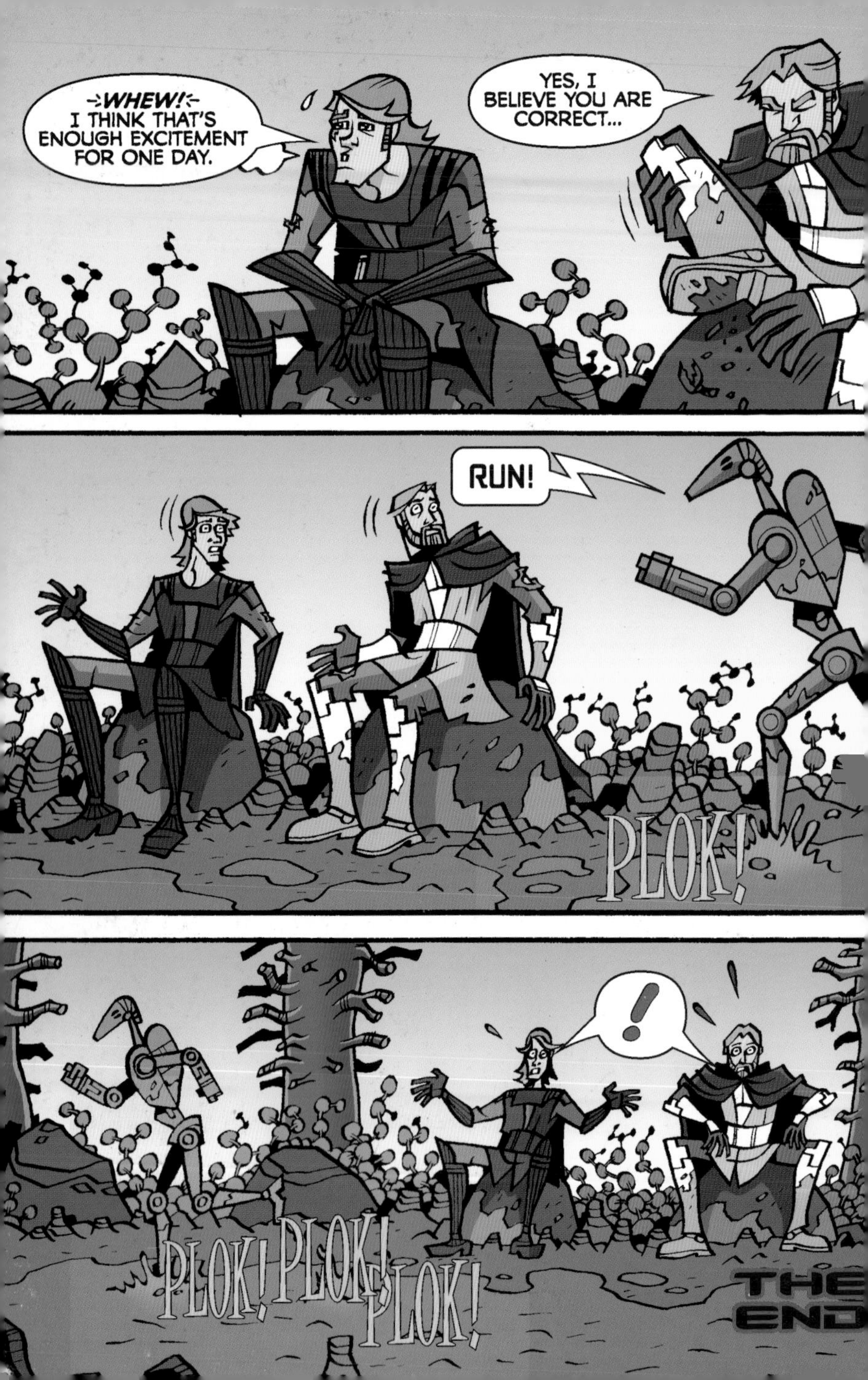

WHEW! I THINK THAT'S ENOUGH EXCITEMENT FOR ONE DAY.
YES, I BELIEVE YOU ARE CORRECT...
RUN!
PLOK!
!
PLOK! PLOK! PLOK!
THE END

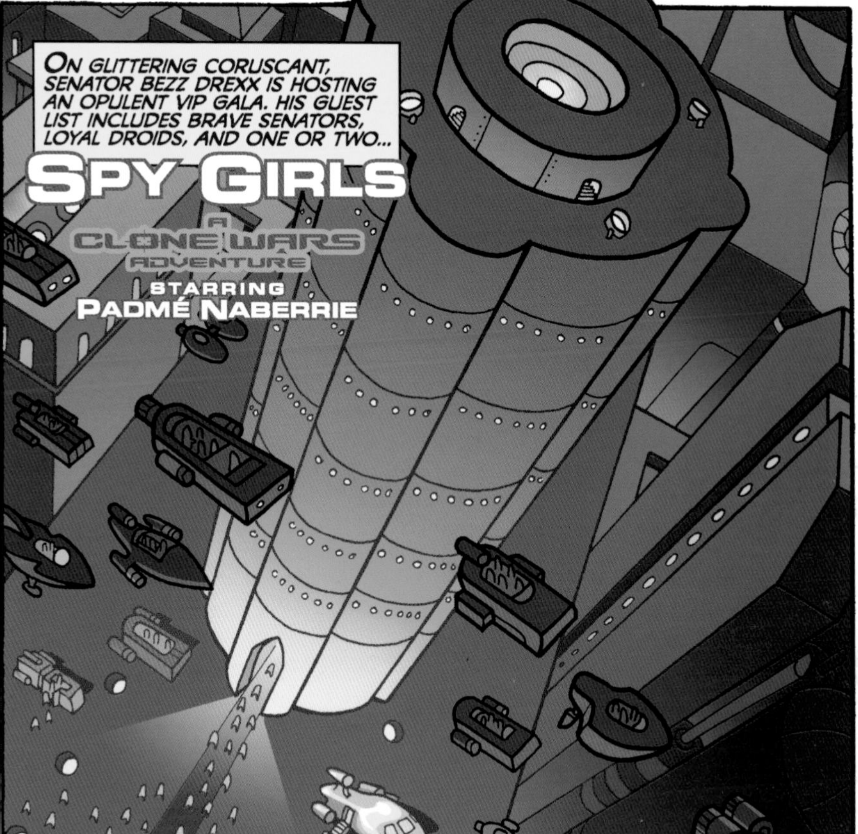
ON GLITTERING CORUSCANT, SENATOR BEZZ DREXX IS HOSTING AN OPULENT VIP GALA. HIS GUEST LIST INCLUDES BRAVE SENATORS, LOYAL DROIDS, AND ONE OR TWO...
SPY GIRLS
A CLONE WARS ADVENTURE
STARRING
PADMÉ NABERRIE

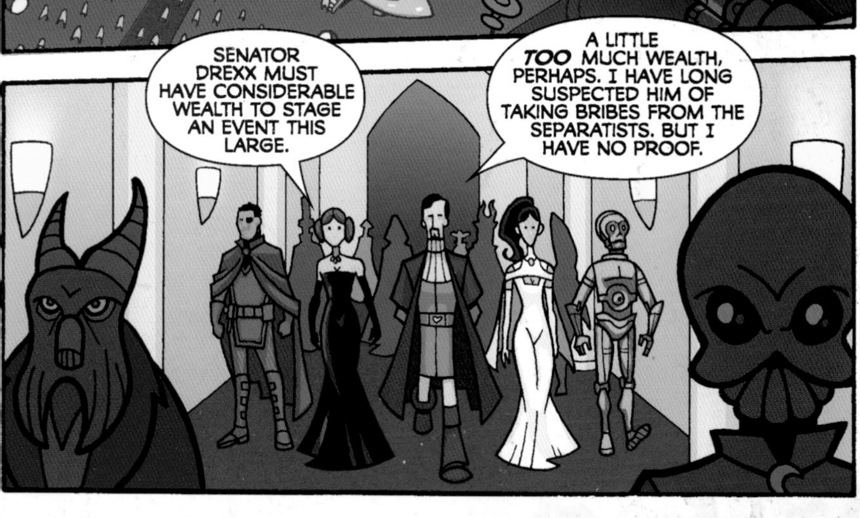
SENATOR DREXX MUST HAVE CONSIDERABLE WEALTH TO STAGE AN EVENT THIS LARGE.
A LITTLE *TOO* MUCH WEALTH, PERHAPS. I HAVE LONG SUSPECTED HIM OF TAKING BRIBES FROM THE SEPARATISTS. BUT I HAVE NO PROOF.

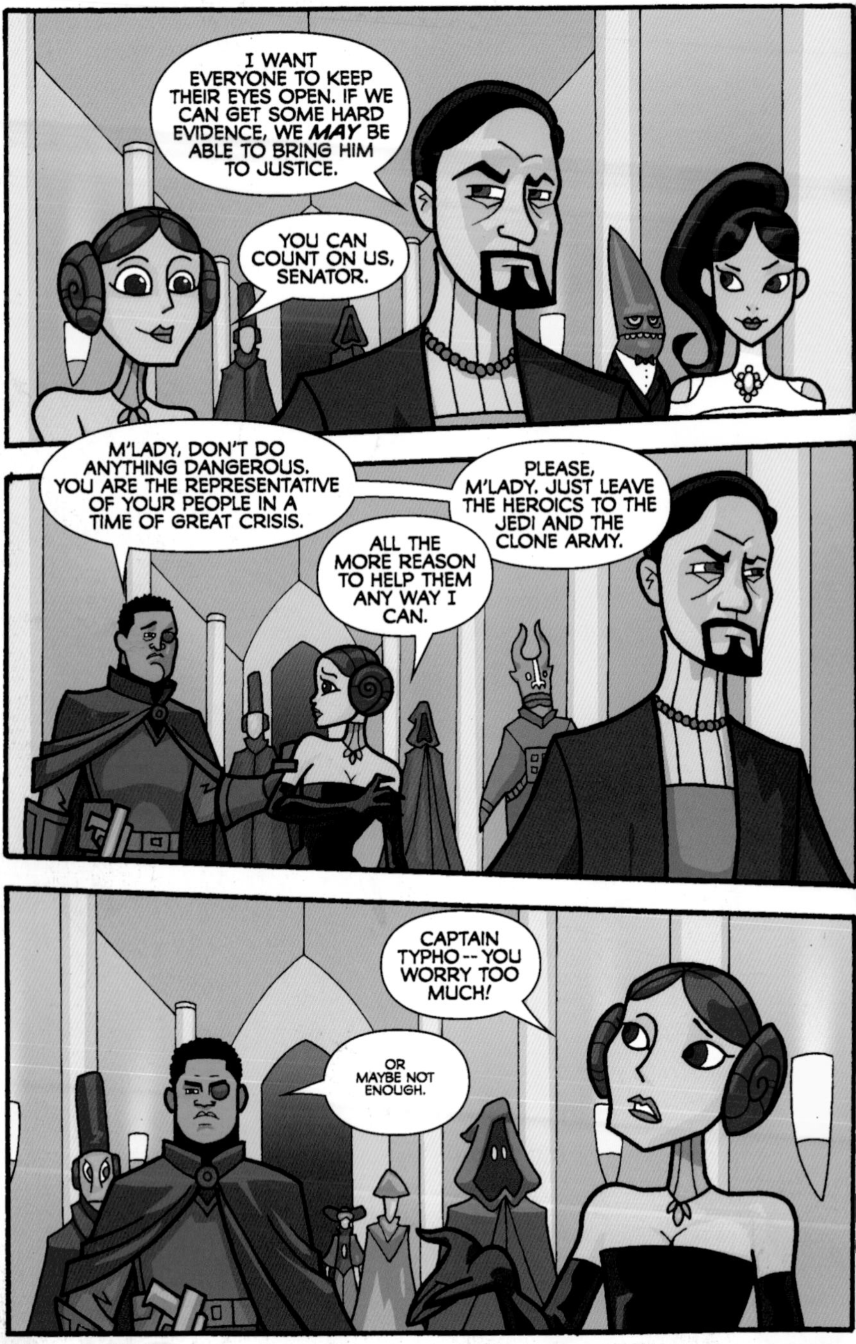
I WANT EVERYONE TO KEEP THEIR EYES OPEN. IF WE CAN GET SOME HARD EVIDENCE, WE *MAY* BE ABLE TO BRING HIM TO JUSTICE.
YOU CAN COUNT ON US, SENATOR.
M'LADY, DON'T DO ANYTHING DANGEROUS. YOU ARE THE REPRESENTATIVE OF YOUR PEOPLE IN A TIME OF GREAT CRISIS.
PLEASE, M'LADY. JUST LEAVE THE HEROICS TO THE JEDI AND THE CLONE ARMY.
ALL THE MORE REASON TO HELP THEM ANY WAY I CAN.
CAPTAIN TYPHO-- YOU WORRY TOO MUCH!
OR MAYBE NOT ENOUGH.

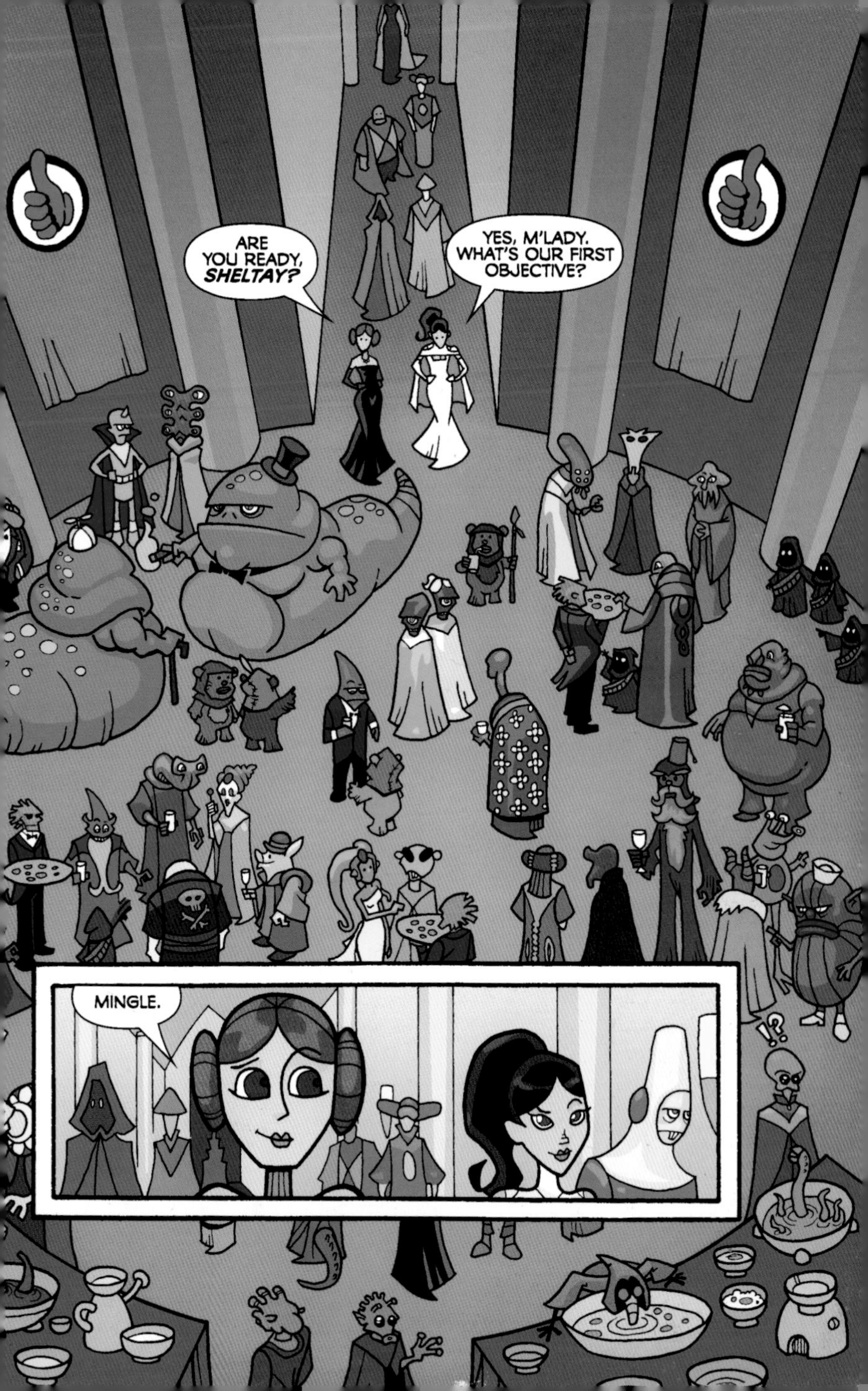
ARE YOU READY, ***SHELTAY?***
YES, M'LADY. WHAT'S OUR FIRST OBJECTIVE?
MINGLE.
!?

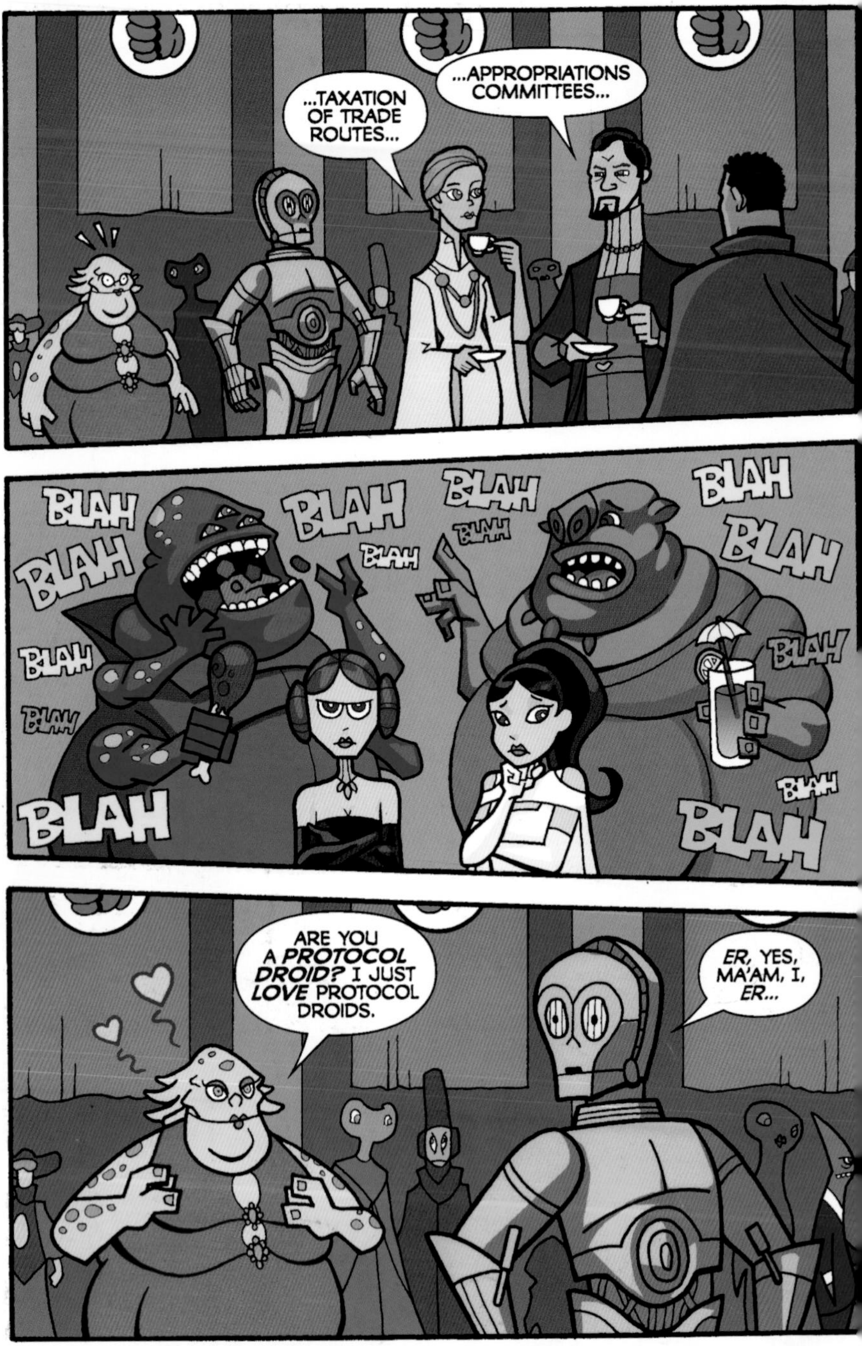

...TAXATION OF TRADE ROUTES...
...APPROPRIATIONS COMMITTEES...
BLAH
BLAH
BLAH
BLAH
BLAH
BLAH
BLAH
BLAH
BLAH
BLAH
BLAH
BLAH
BLAH
BLAH
BLAH
ARE YOU A *PROTOCOL DROID?* I JUST *LOVE* PROTOCOL DROIDS.
ER, YES, MA'AM, I, *ER...*

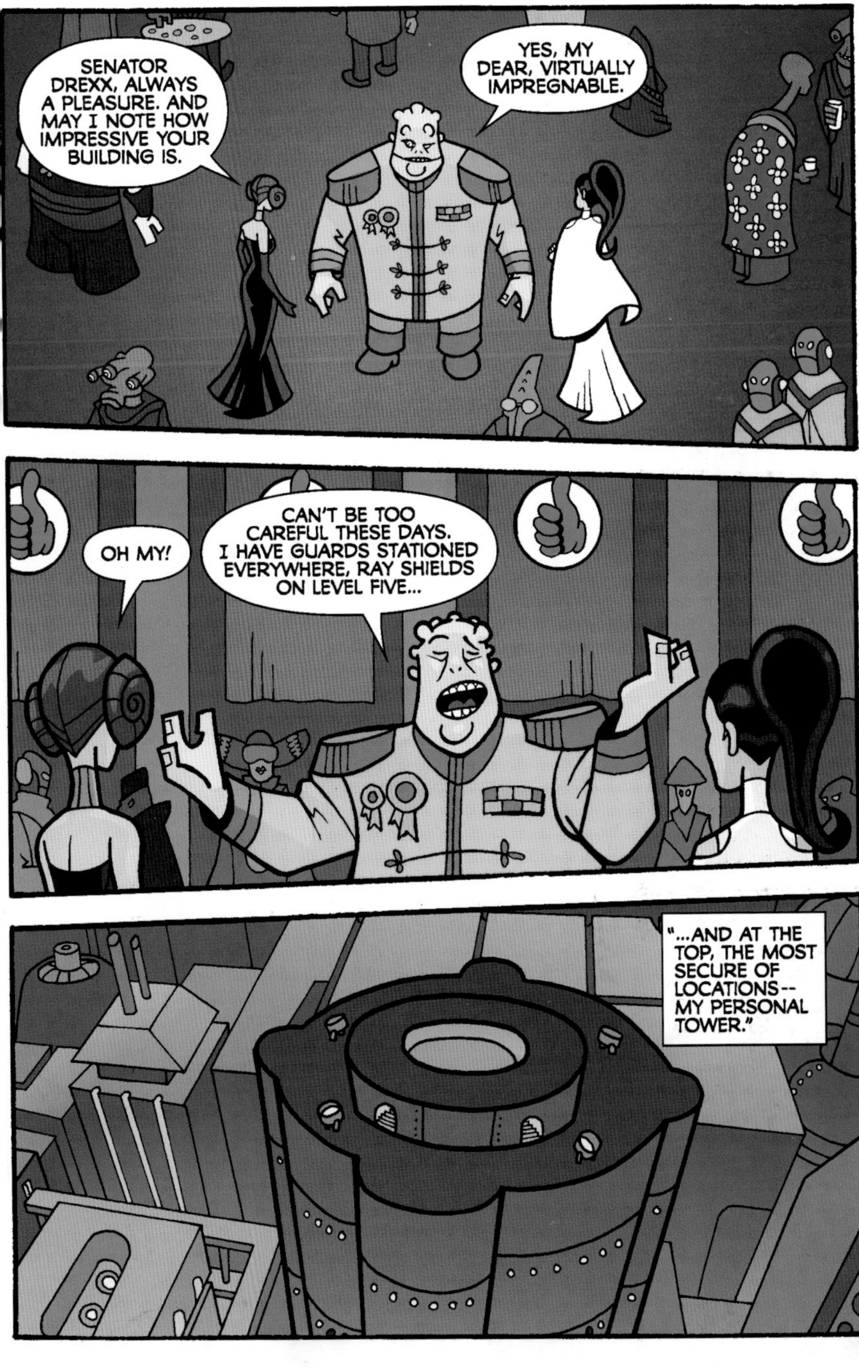
SENATOR DREXX, ALWAYS A PLEASURE. AND MAY I NOTE HOW IMPRESSIVE YOUR BUILDING IS.
YES, MY DEAR, VIRTUALLY IMPREGNABLE.
OH MY!
CAN'T BE TOO CAREFUL THESE DAYS. I HAVE GUARDS STATIONED EVERYWHERE, RAY SHIELDS ON LEVEL FIVE...
"...AND AT THE TOP, THE MOST SECURE OF LOCATIONS-- MY PERSONAL TOWER."

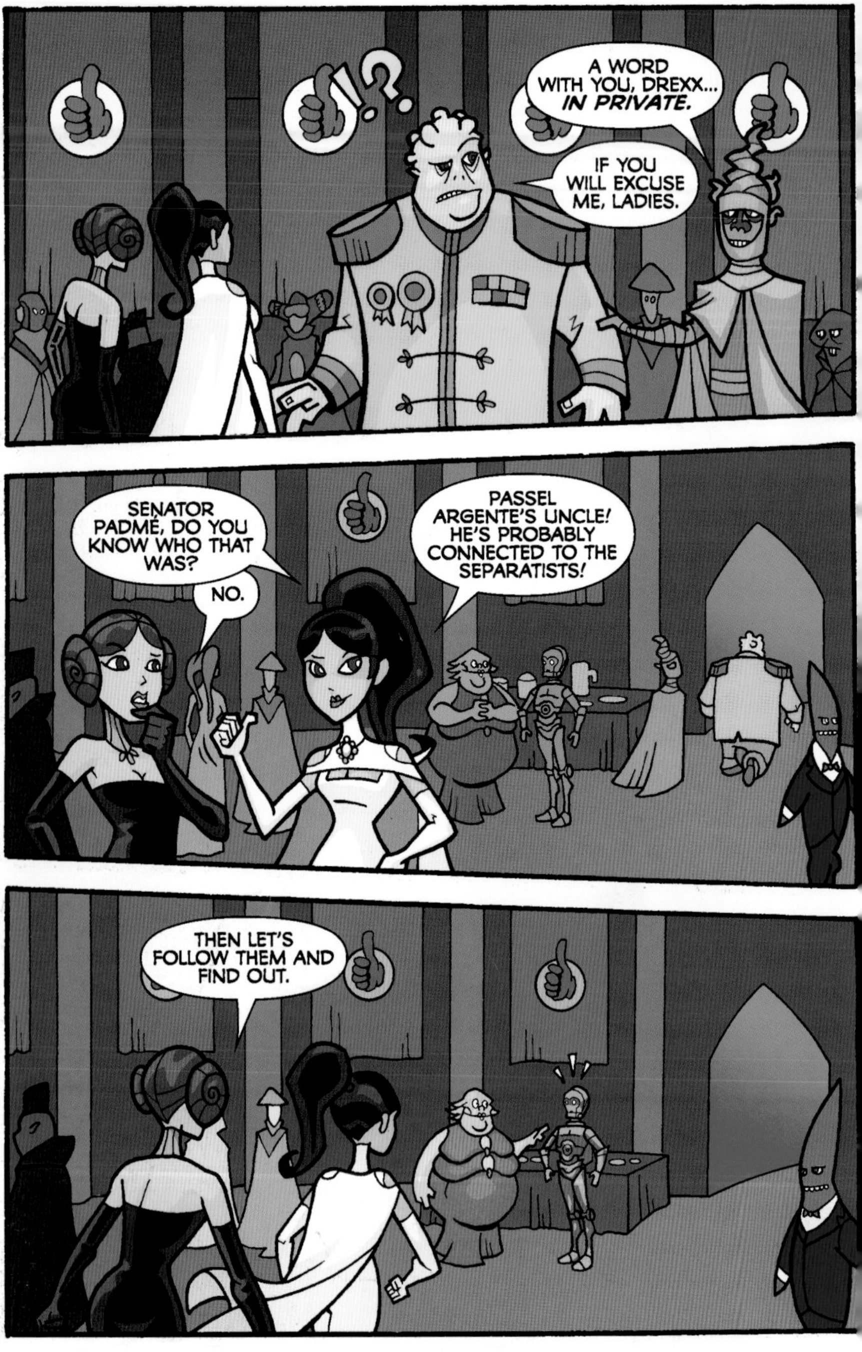
!?
A WORD WITH YOU, DREXX... IN PRIVATE.
IF YOU WILL EXCUSE ME, LADIES.
SENATOR PADMÉ, DO YOU KNOW WHO THAT WAS?
NO.
PASSEL ARGENTE'S UNCLE! HE'S PROBABLY CONNECTED TO THE SEPARATISTS!
THEN LET'S FOLLOW THEM AND FIND OUT.

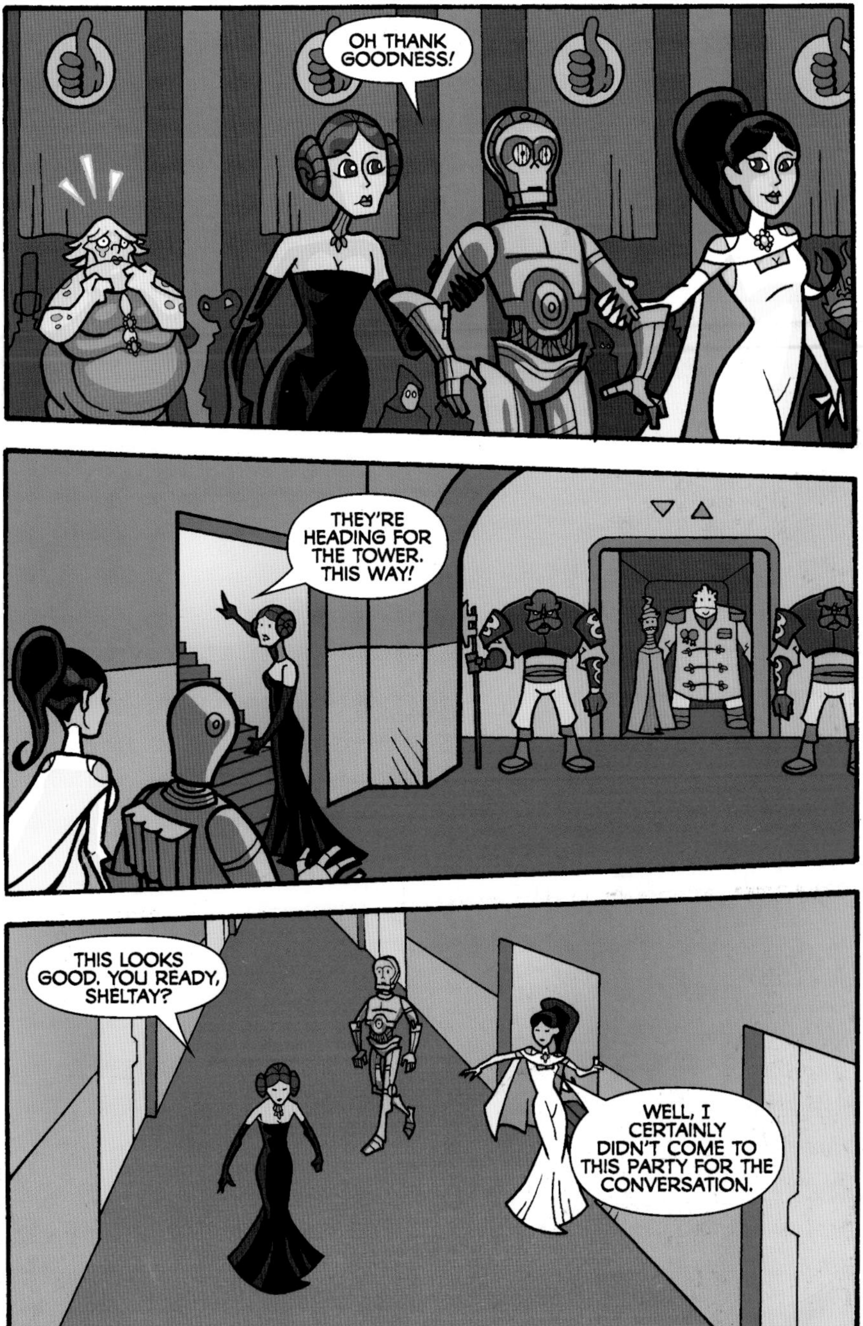
OH THANK GOODNESS!
THEY'RE HEADING FOR THE TOWER. THIS WAY!
THIS LOOKS GOOD. YOU READY, SHELTAY?
WELL, I CERTAINLY DIDN'T COME TO THIS PARTY FOR THE CONVERSATION.

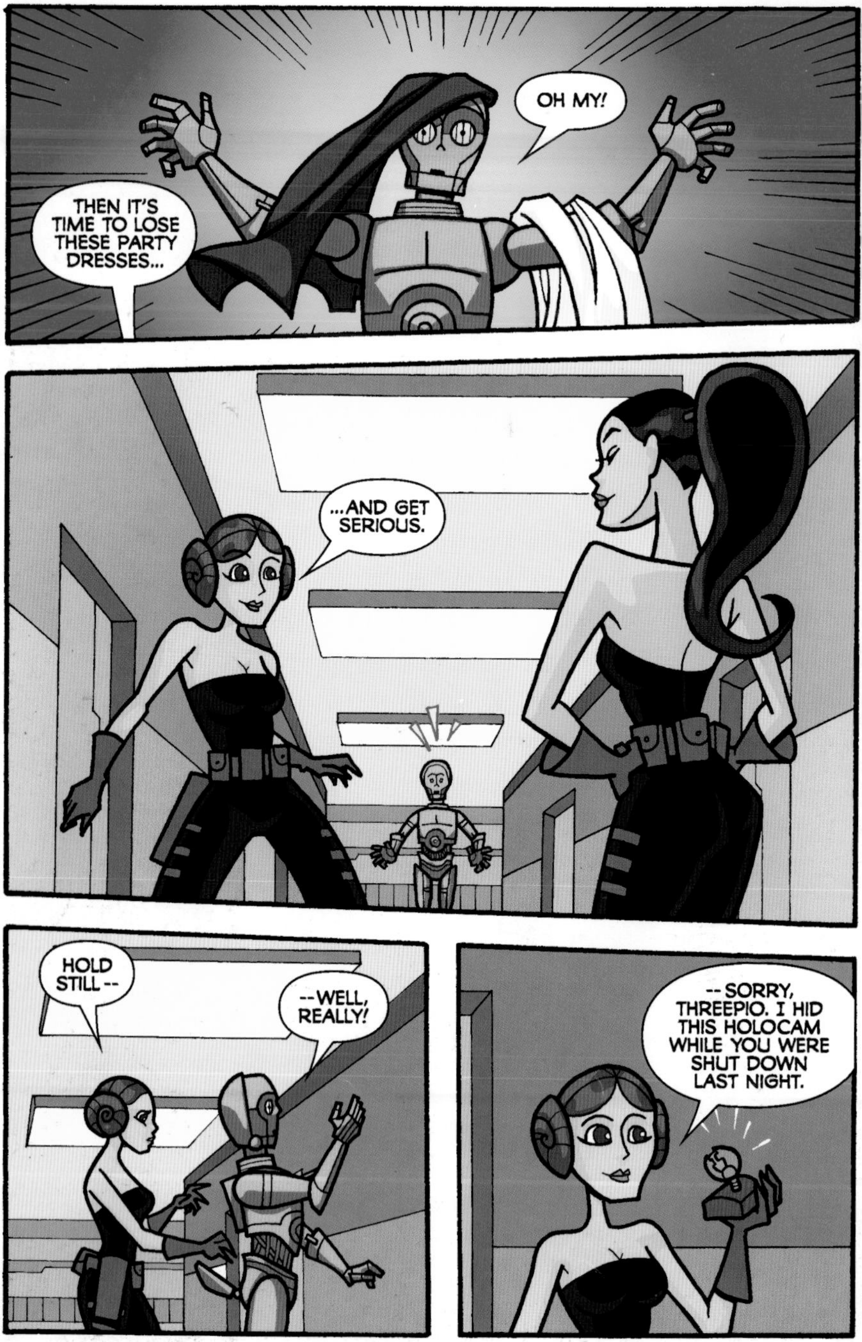
OH MY!
THEN IT'S TIME TO LOSE THESE PARTY DRESSES...
...AND GET SERIOUS.
HOLD STILL --
--WELL, REALLY!
-- SORRY, THREEPIO. I HID THIS HOLOCAM WHILE YOU WERE SHUT DOWN LAST NIGHT.

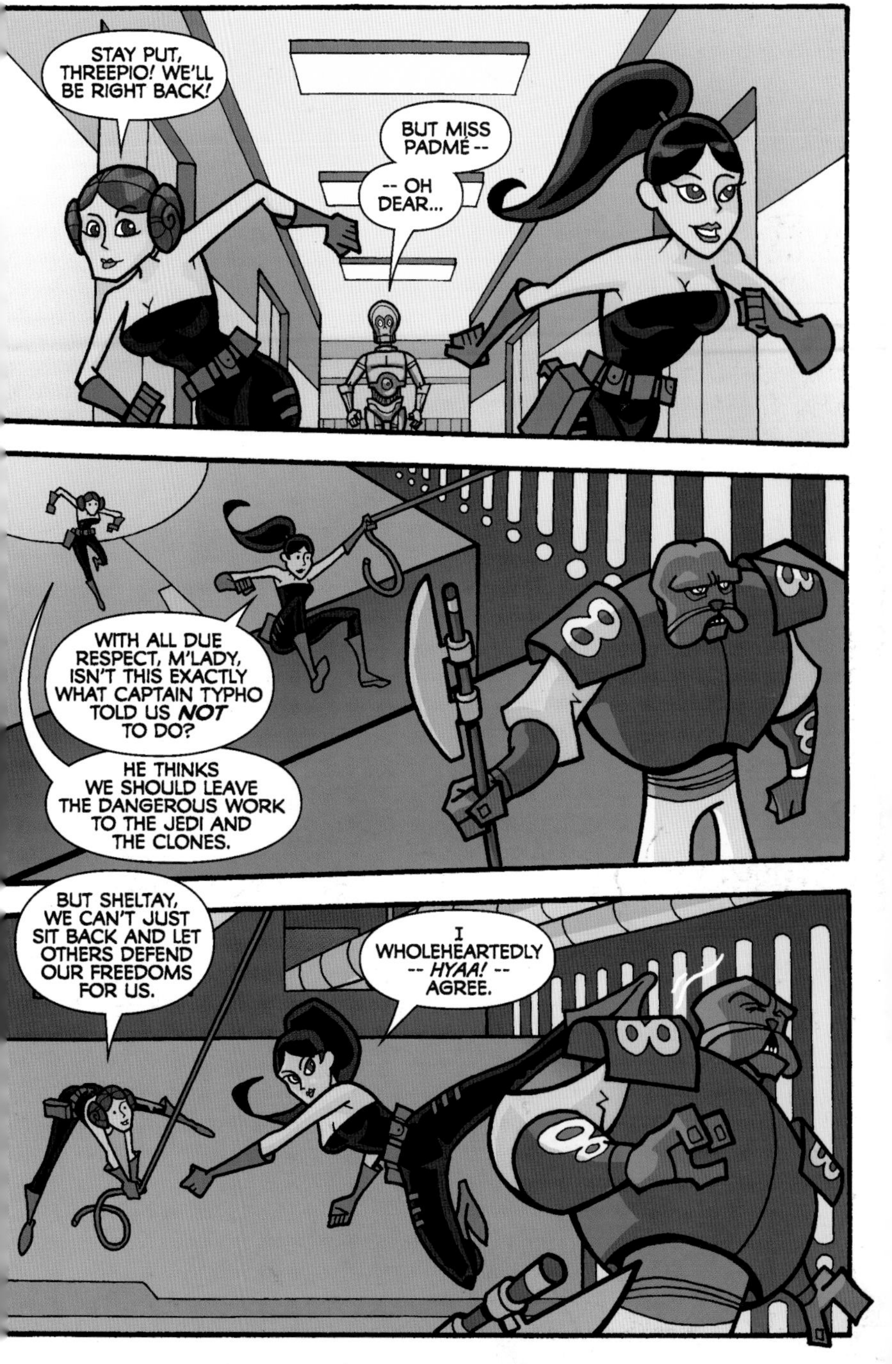
STAY PUT, THREEPIO! WE'LL BE RIGHT BACK!
BUT MISS PADMÉ --
-- OH DEAR...
WITH ALL DUE RESPECT, M'LADY, ISN'T THIS EXACTLY WHAT CAPTAIN TYPHO TOLD US *NOT* TO DO?
HE THINKS WE SHOULD LEAVE THE DANGEROUS WORK TO THE JEDI AND THE CLONES.
BUT SHELTAY, WE CAN'T JUST SIT BACK AND LET OTHERS DEFEND OUR FREEDOMS FOR US.
I WHOLEHEARTEDLY -- *HYAA!* -- AGREE.

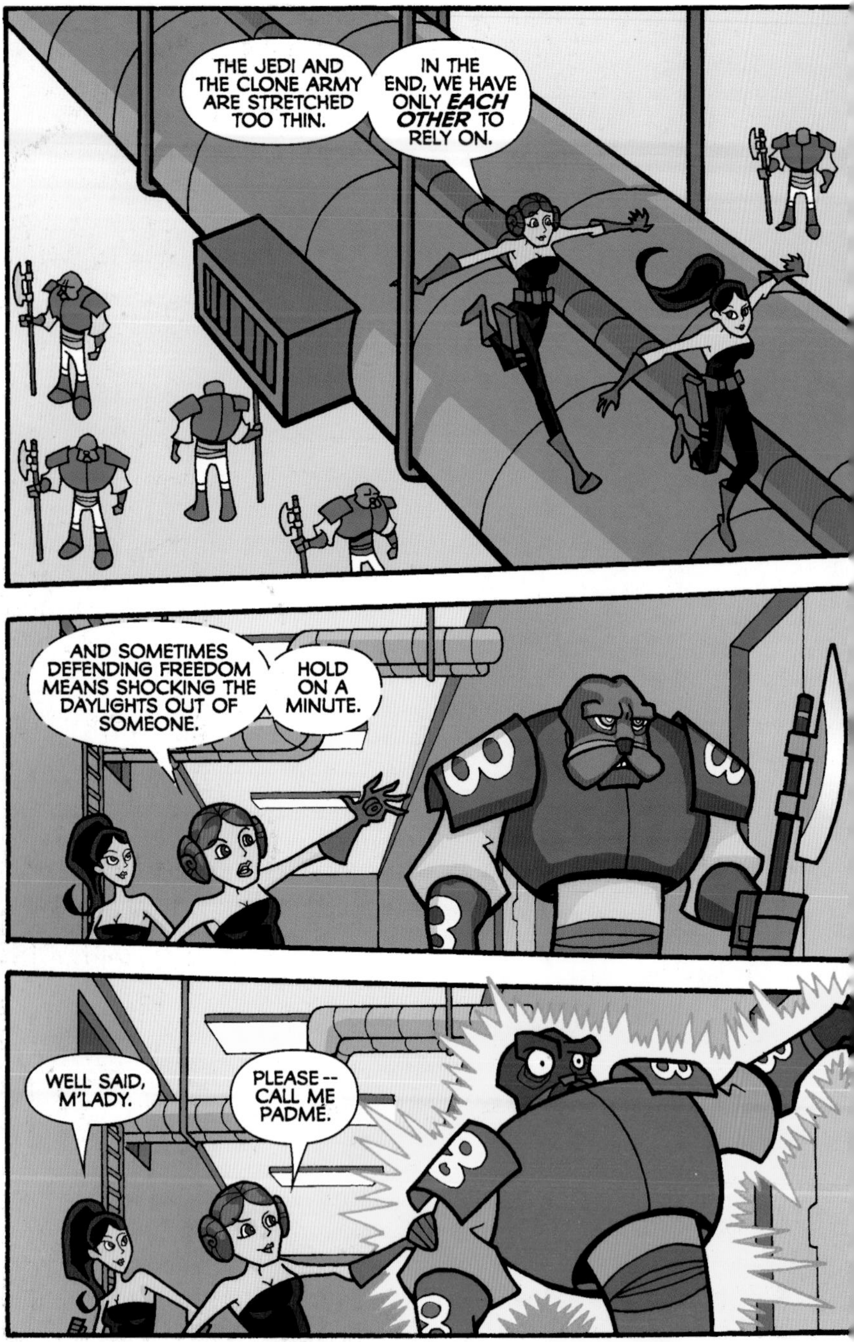
THE JEDI AND THE CLONE ARMY ARE STRETCHED TOO THIN.
IN THE END, WE HAVE ONLY *EACH OTHER* TO RELY ON.
AND SOMETIMES DEFENDING FREEDOM MEANS SHOCKING THE DAYLIGHTS OUT OF SOMEONE.
HOLD ON A MINUTE.
WELL SAID, M'LADY.
PLEASE -- CALL ME PADMÉ.

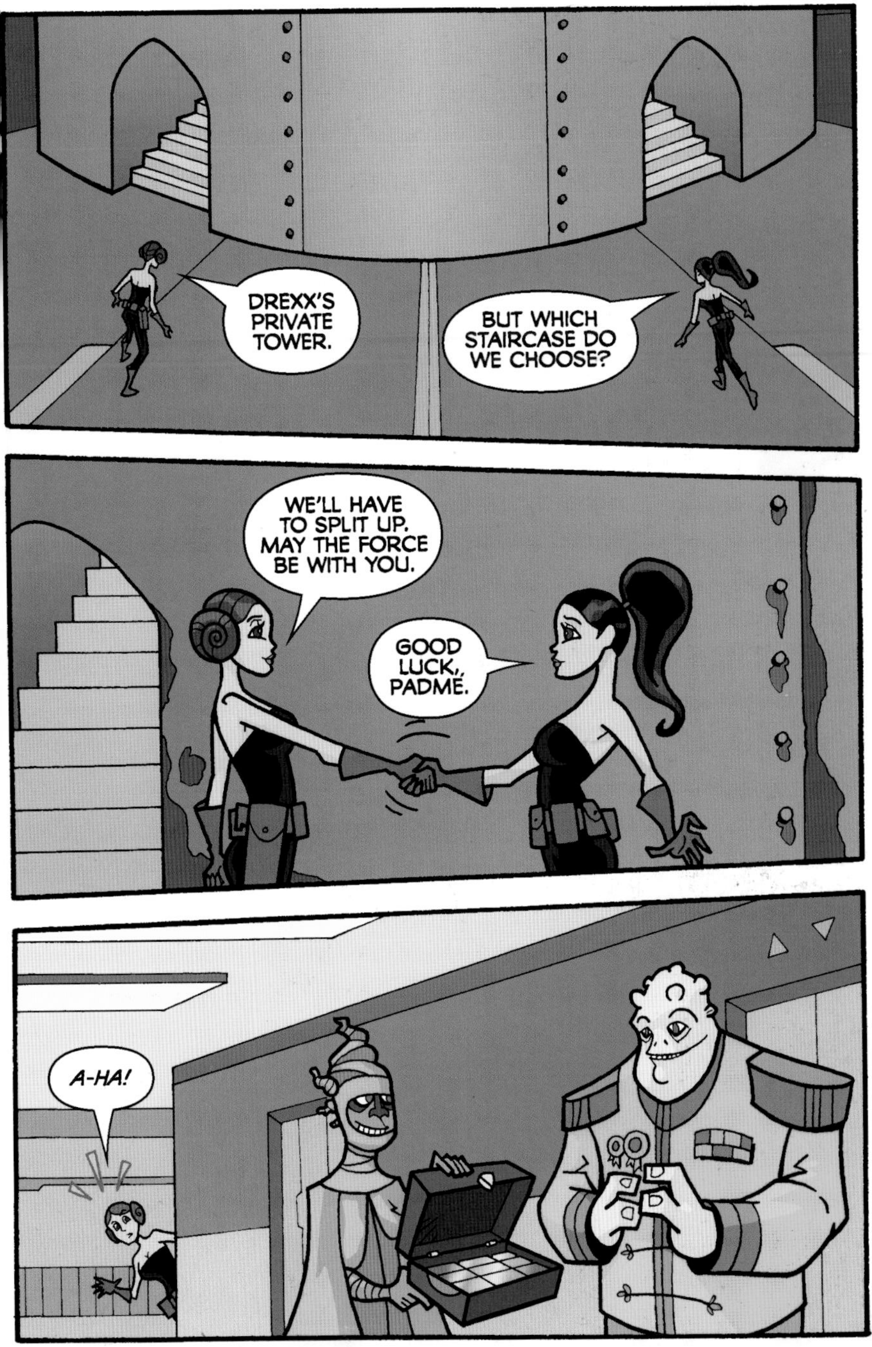
DREXX'S PRIVATE TOWER.
BUT WHICH STAIRCASE DO WE CHOOSE?
WE'LL HAVE TO SPLIT UP. MAY THE FORCE BE WITH YOU.
GOOD LUCK,, PADMÉ.
A-HA!

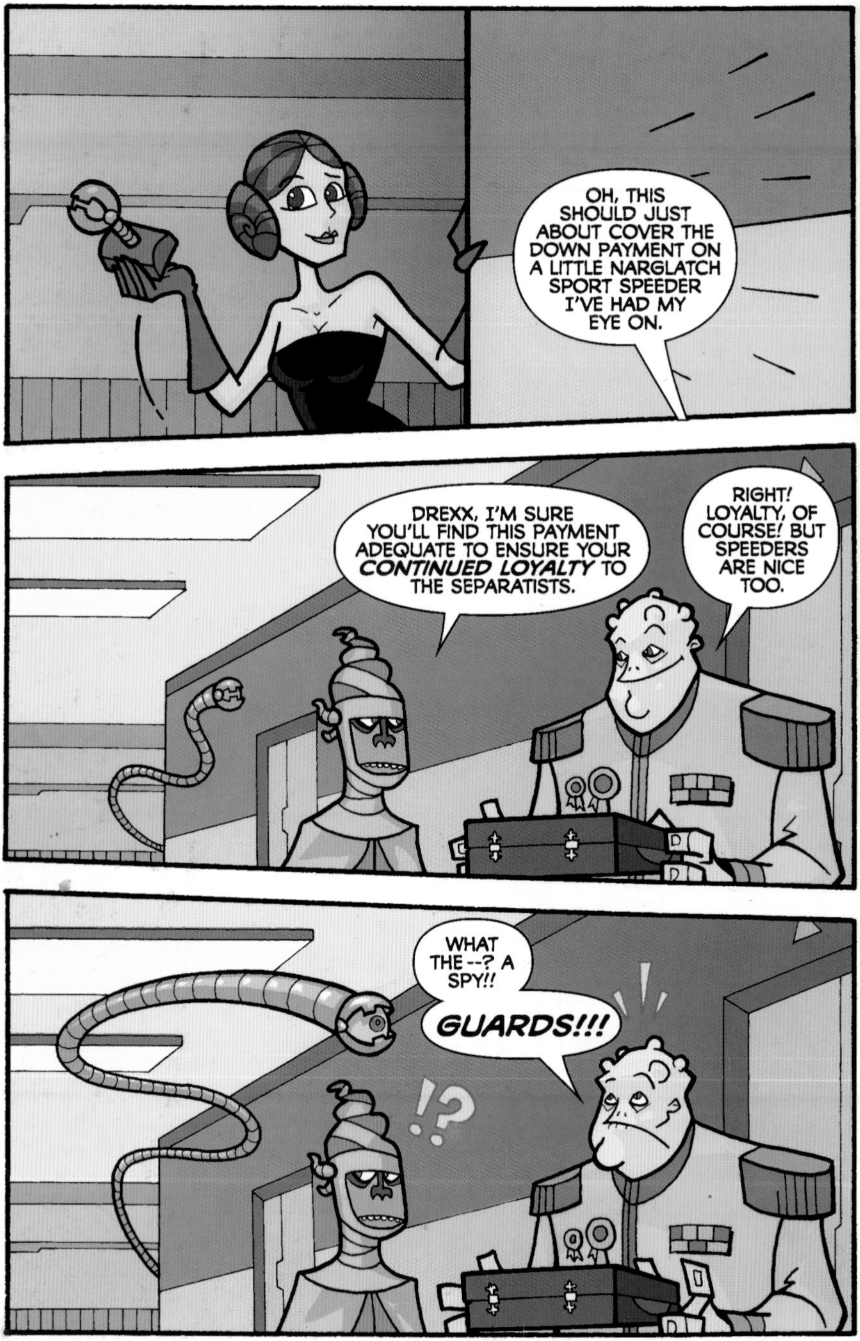
OH, THIS SHOULD JUST ABOUT COVER THE DOWN PAYMENT ON A LITTLE NARGLATCH SPORT SPEEDER I'VE HAD MY EYE ON.
DREXX, I'M SURE YOU'LL FIND THIS PAYMENT ADEQUATE TO ENSURE YOUR *CONTINUED LOYALTY* TO THE SEPARATISTS.
RIGHT! LOYALTY, OF COURSE! BUT SPEEDERS ARE NICE TOO.
WHAT THE --? A SPY!!
GUARDS!!!
!?

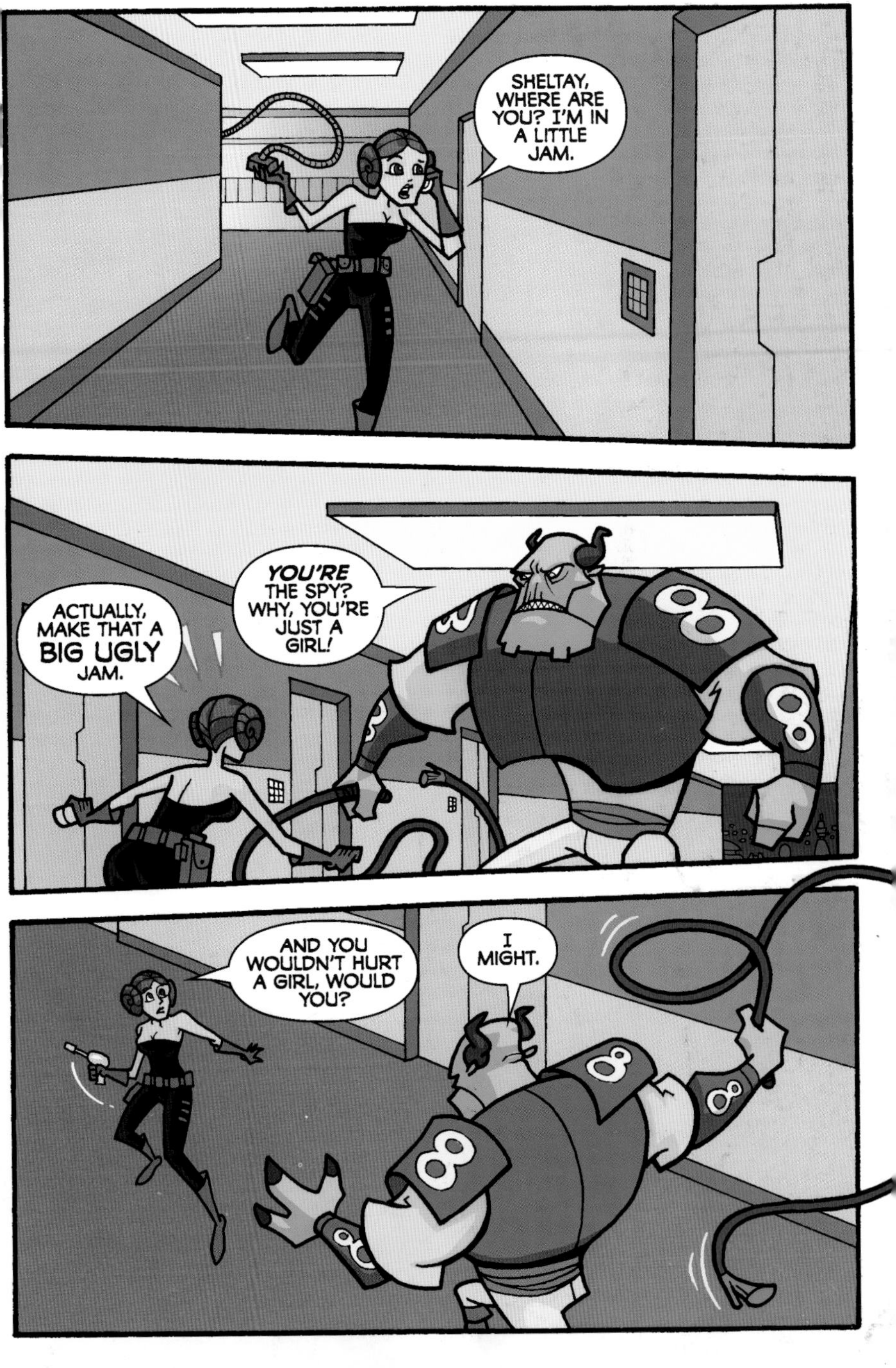
SHELTAY, WHERE ARE YOU? I'M IN A LITTLE JAM.
ACTUALLY, MAKE THAT A BIG UGLY JAM.
YOU'RE THE SPY? WHY, YOU'RE JUST A GIRL!
AND YOU WOULDN'T HURT A GIRL, WOULD YOU?
I MIGHT.

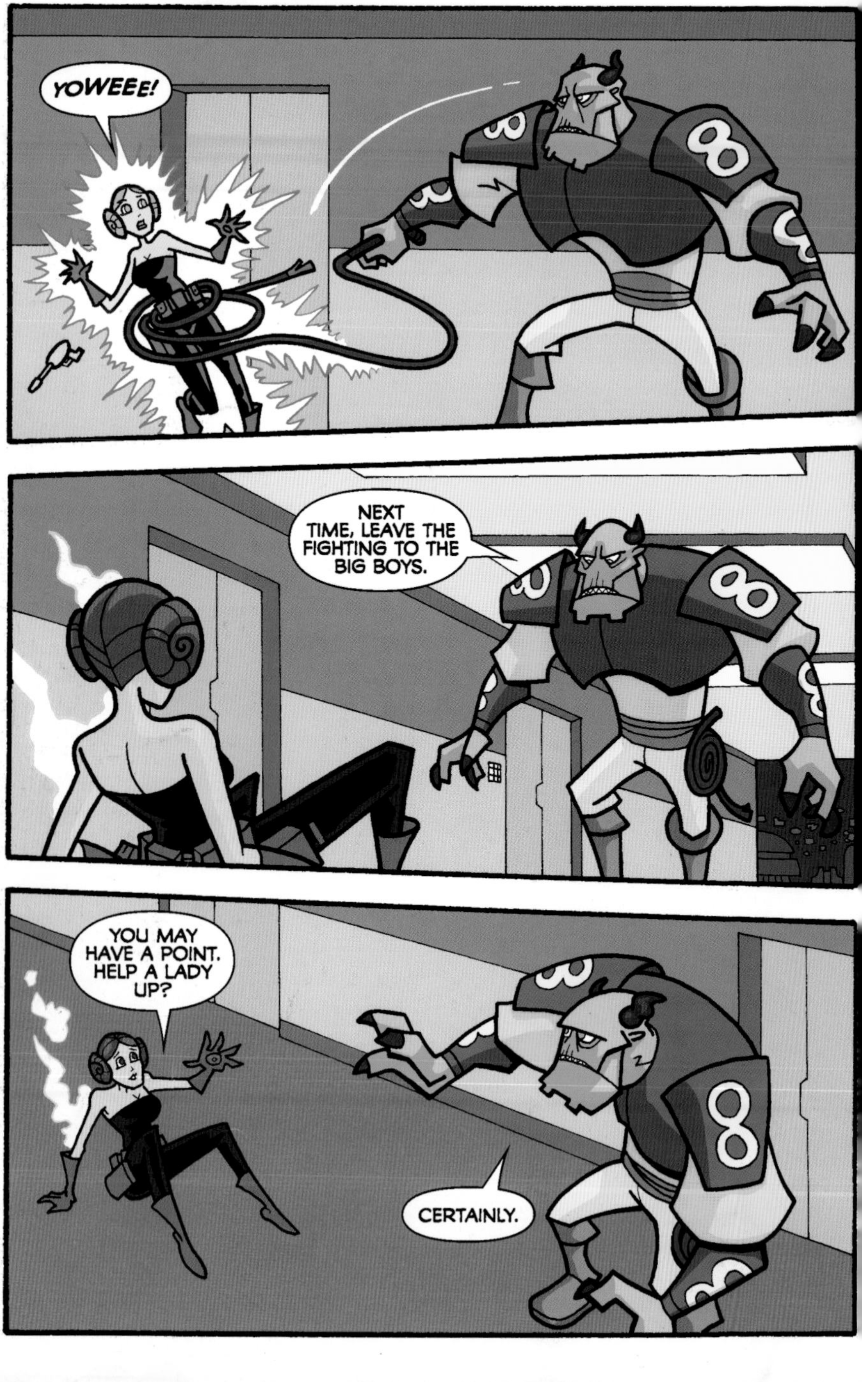
YOWEEE!
NEXT TIME, LEAVE THE FIGHTING TO THE BIG BOYS.
YOU MAY HAVE A POINT. HELP A LADY UP?
CERTAINLY.

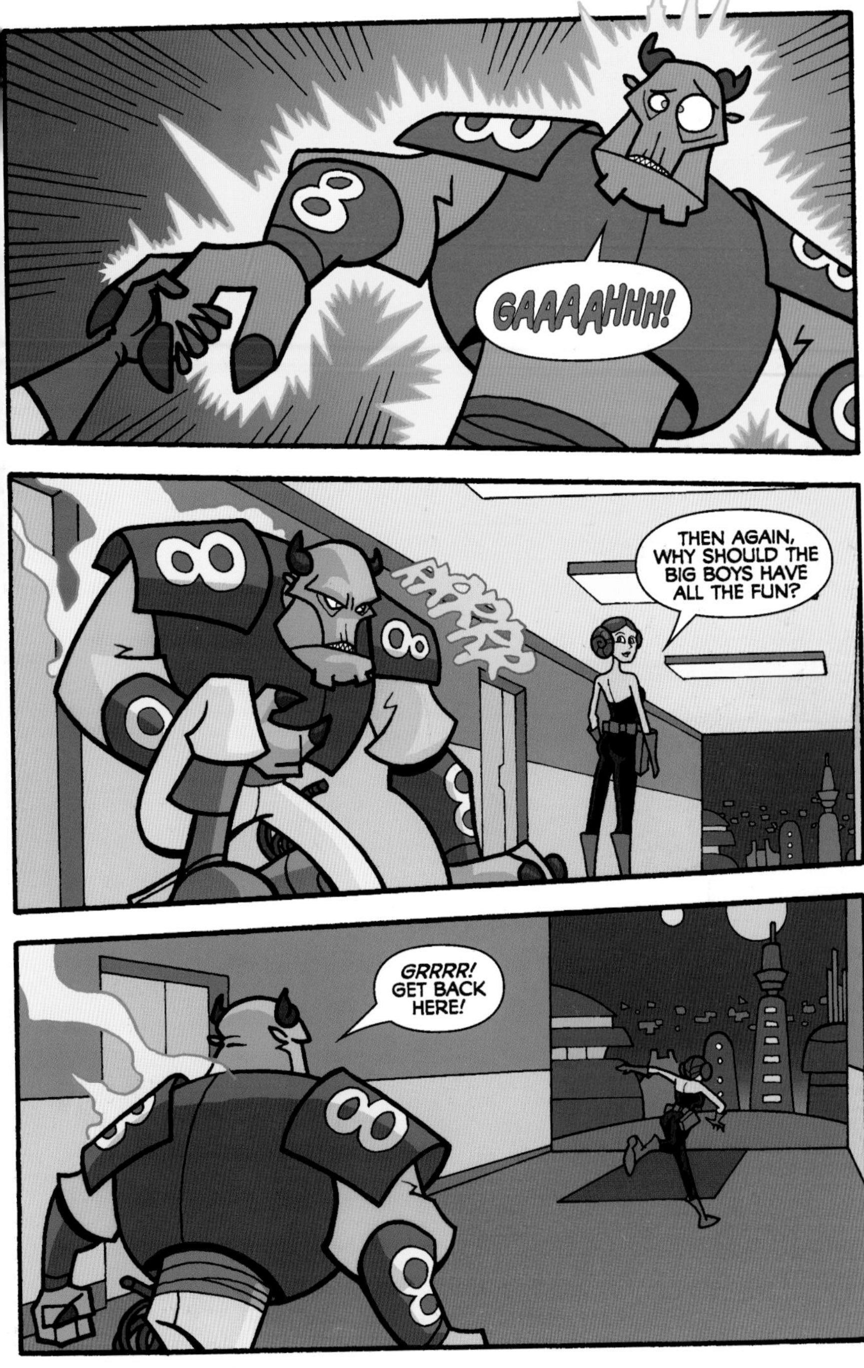

GAAAAHHH!
THEN AGAIN, WHY SHOULD THE BIG BOYS HAVE ALL THE FUN?
GRRRR! GET BACK HERE!

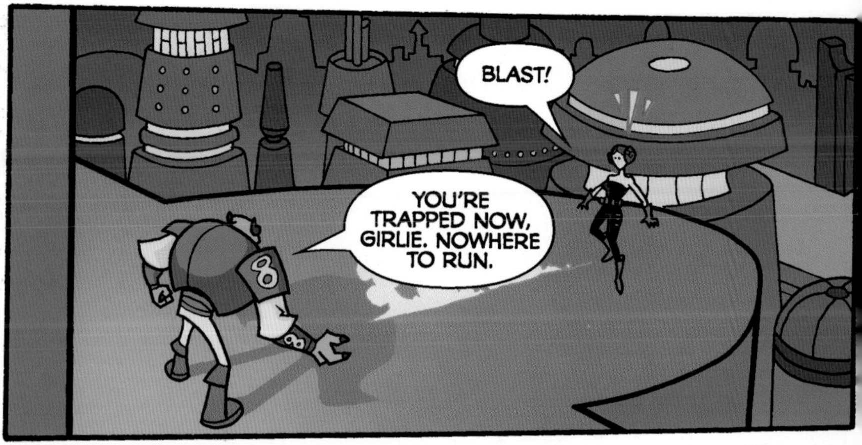
BLAST!
YOU'RE TRAPPED NOW, GIRLIE. NOWHERE TO RUN.

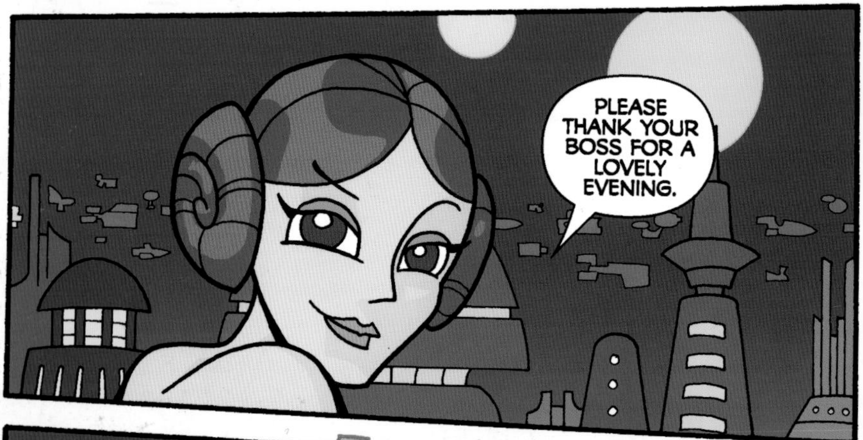
PLEASE THANK YOUR BOSS FOR A LOVELY EVENING.

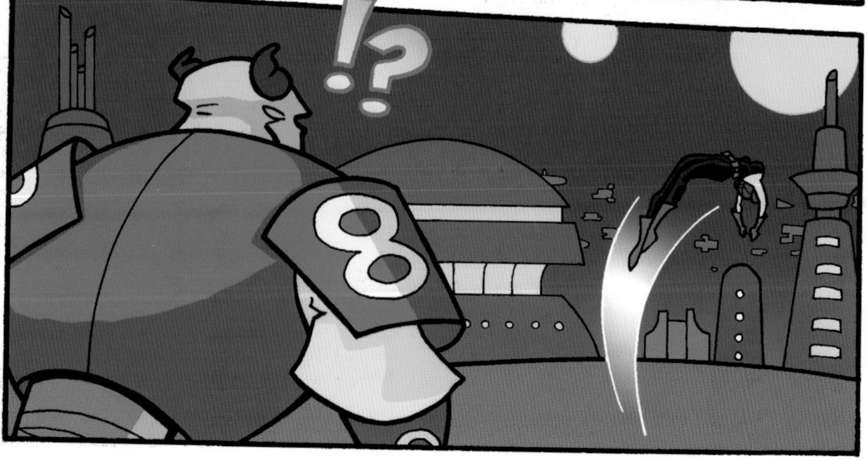
!?

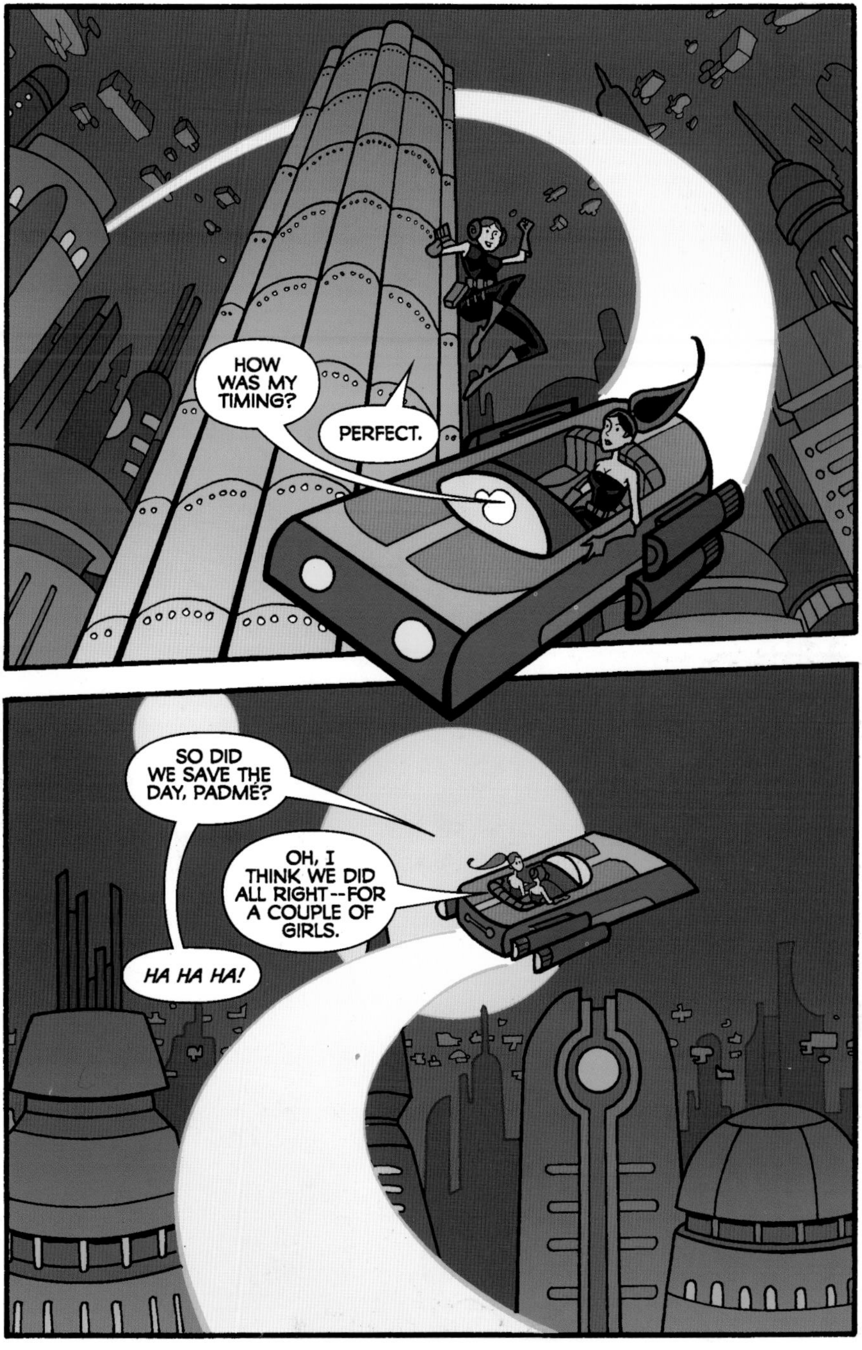
HOW WAS MY TIMING?
PERFECT.
SO DID WE SAVE THE DAY, PADMÉ?
OH, I THINK WE DID ALL RIGHT--FOR A COUPLE OF GIRLS.
HA HA HA!

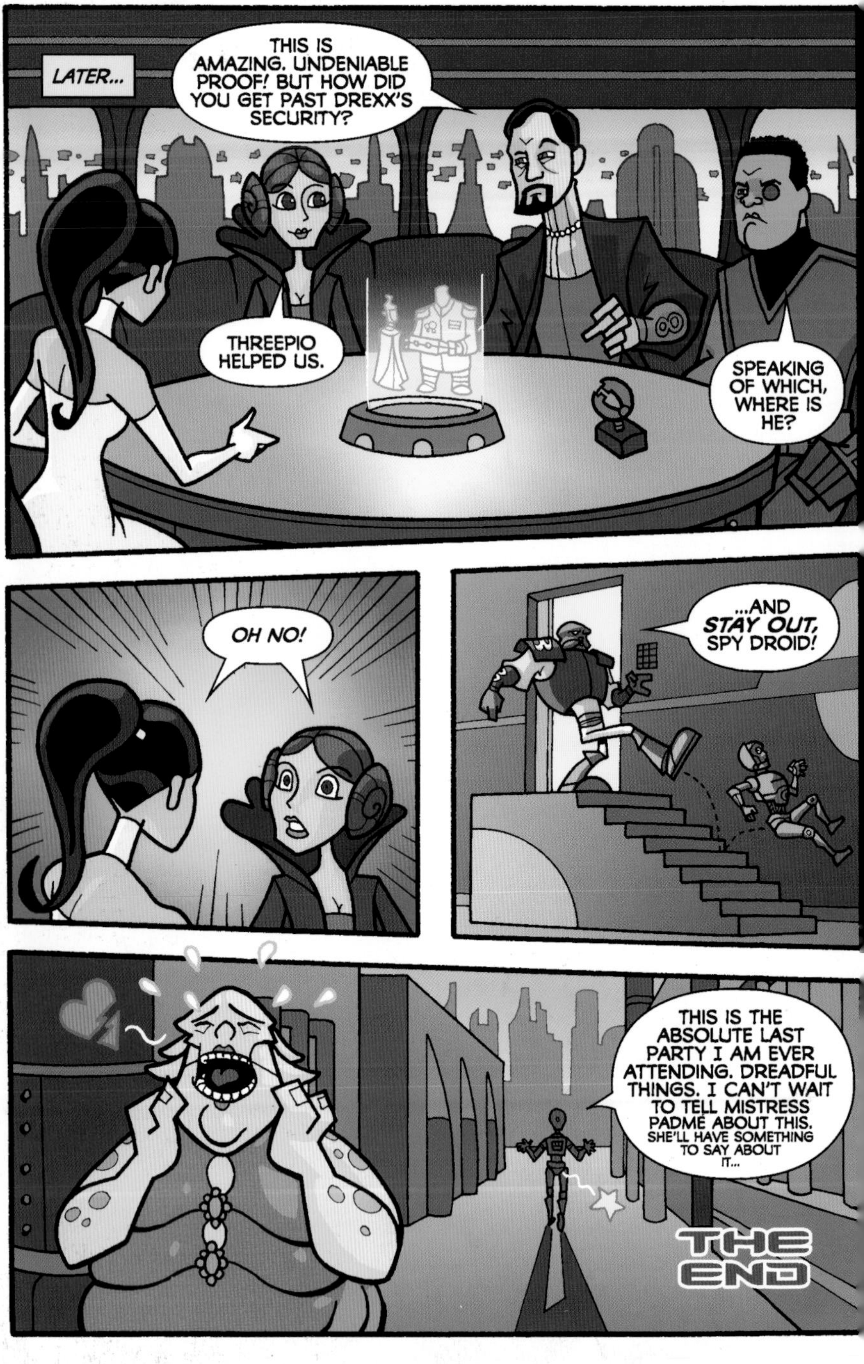
LATER...
THIS IS AMAZING. UNDENIABLE PROOF! BUT HOW DID YOU GET PAST DREXX'S SECURITY?
THREEPIO HELPED US.
SPEAKING OF WHICH, WHERE IS HE?
OH NO!
...AND STAY OUT, SPY DROID!
THIS IS THE ABSOLUTE LAST PARTY I AM EVER ATTENDING. DREADFUL THINGS. I CAN'T WAIT TO TELL MISTRESS PADMÉ ABOUT THIS. SHE'LL HAVE SOMETHING TO SAY ABOUT IT...
THE END

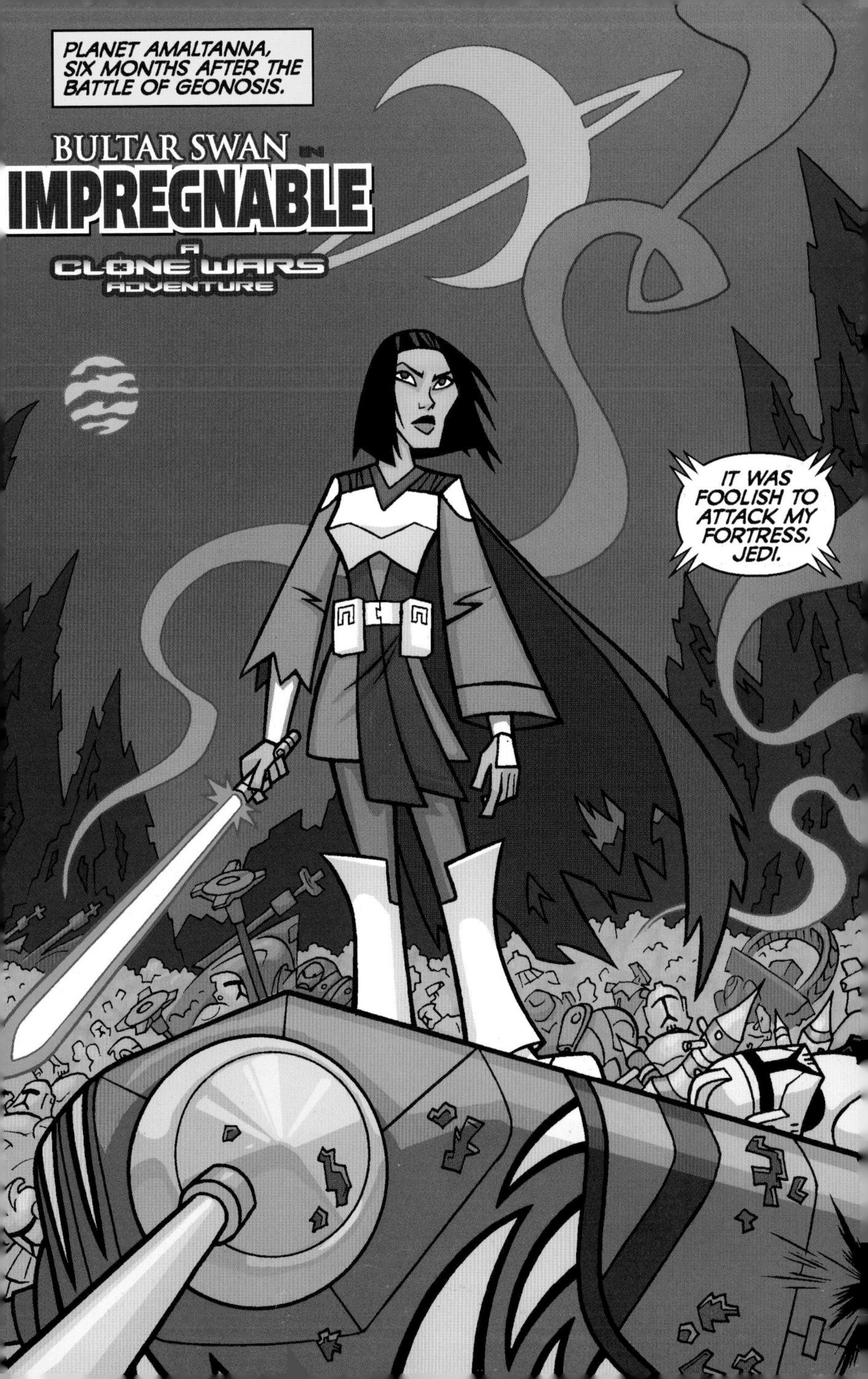
PLANET AMALTANNA, SIX MONTHS AFTER THE BATTLE OF GEONOSIS.
BULTAR SWAN IN
IMPREGNABLE
A CLONE WARS ADVENTURE
IT WAS FOOLISH TO ATTACK MY FORTRESS, JEDI.

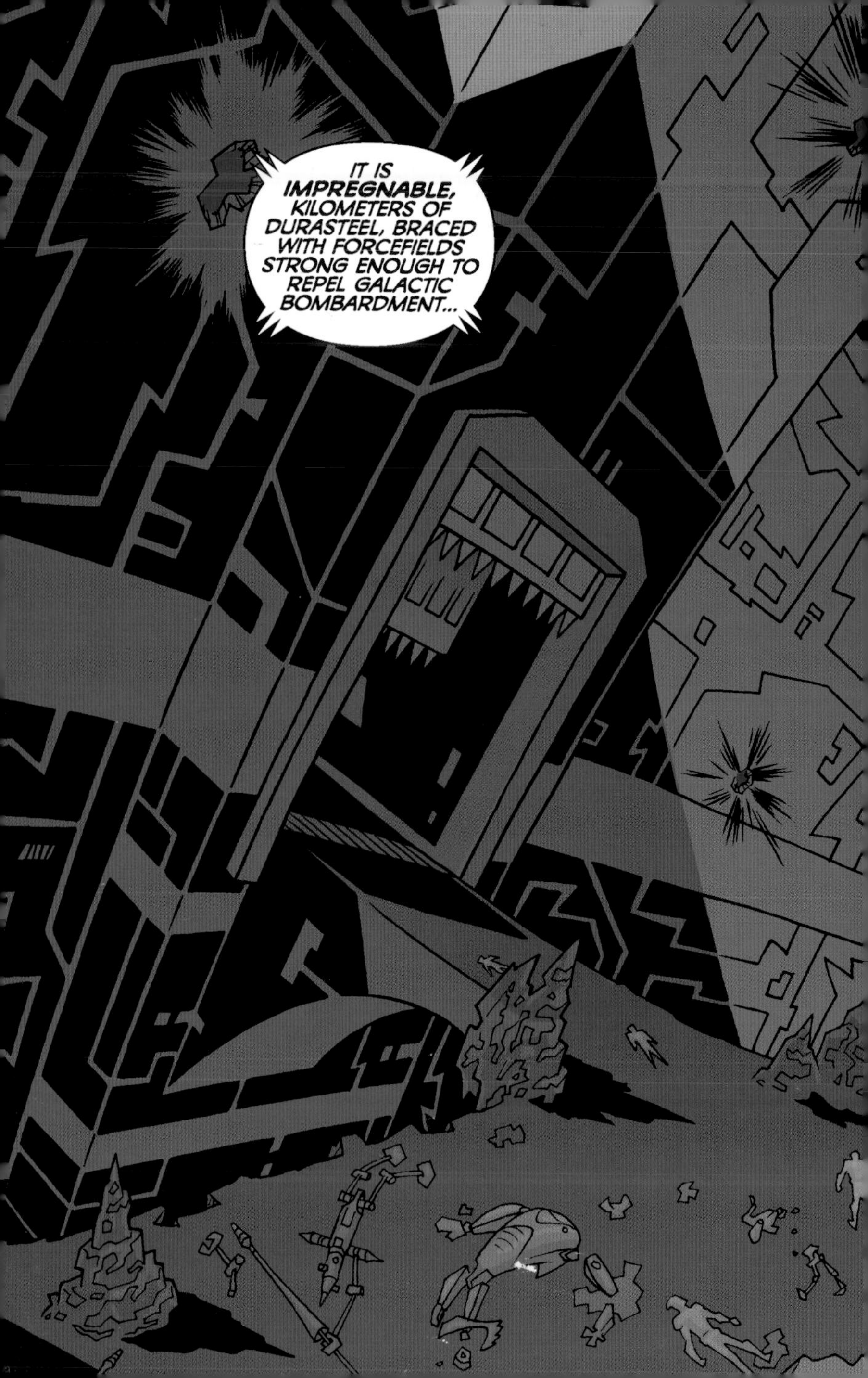
IT IS IMPREGNABLE, KILOMETERS OF DURASTEEL, BRACED WITH FORCEFIELDS STRONG ENOUGH TO REPEL GALACTIC BOMBARDMENT...

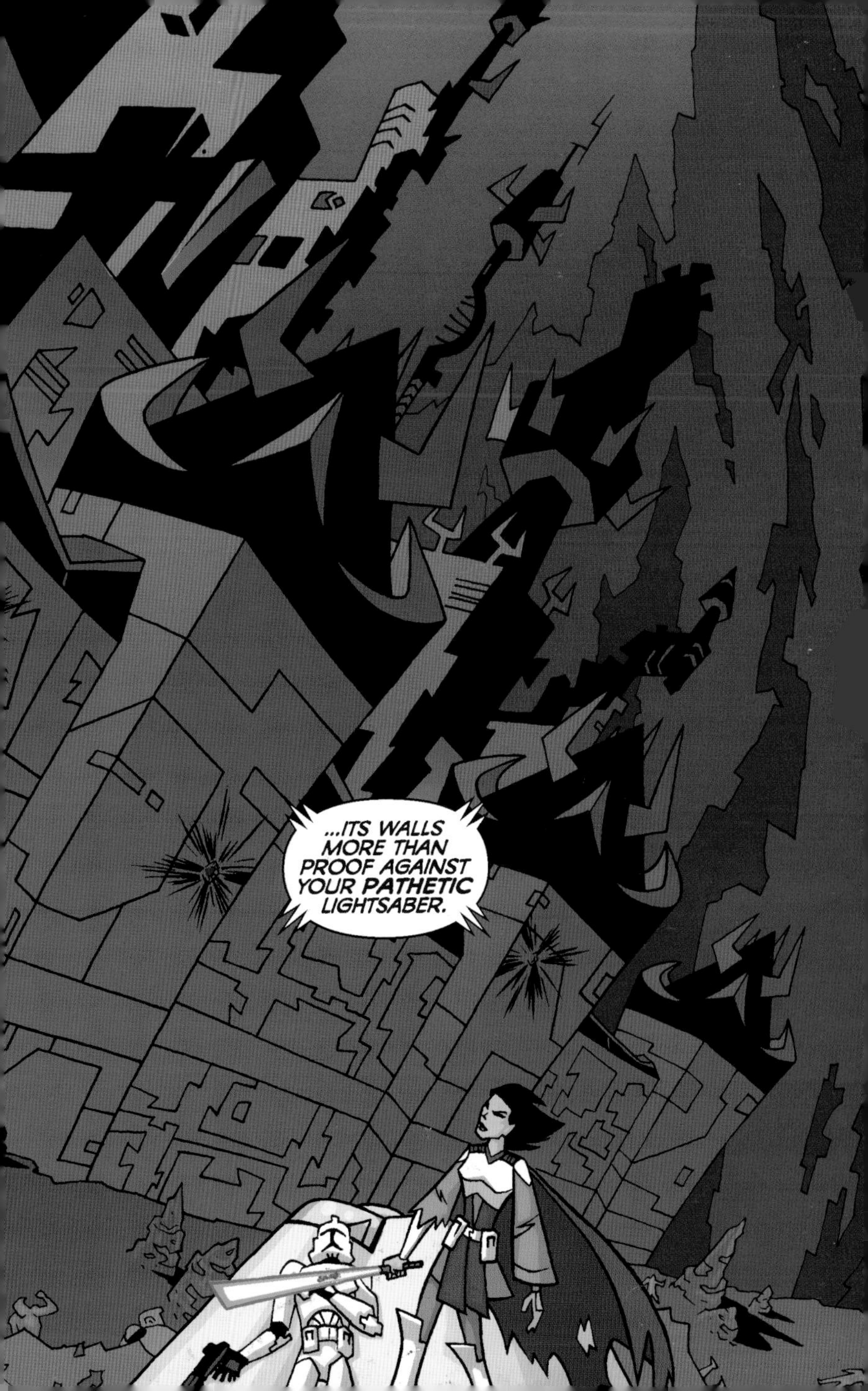
...ITS WALLS MORE THAN PROOF AGAINST YOUR PATHETIC LIGHTSABER.

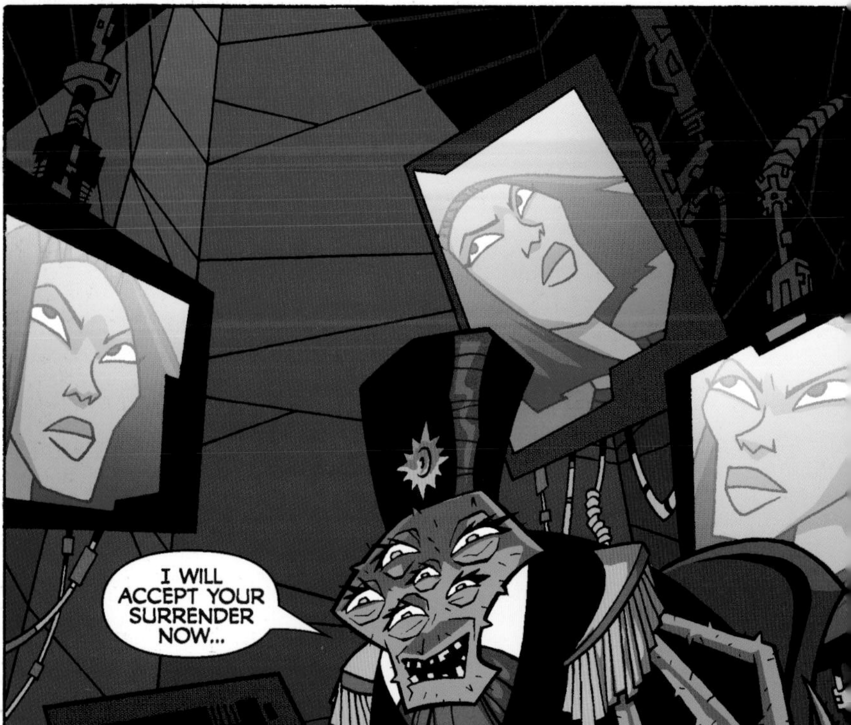
I WILL ACCEPT YOUR SURRENDER NOW...

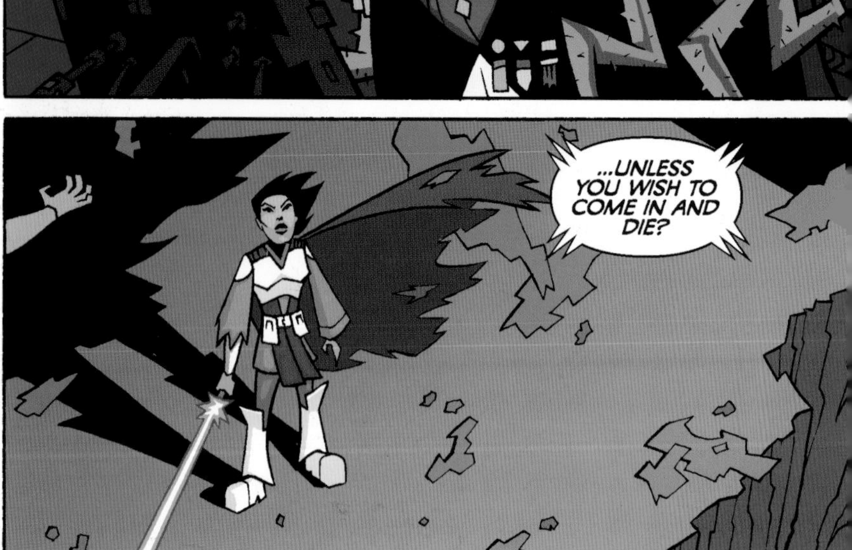
...UNLESS YOU WISH TO COME IN AND DIE?

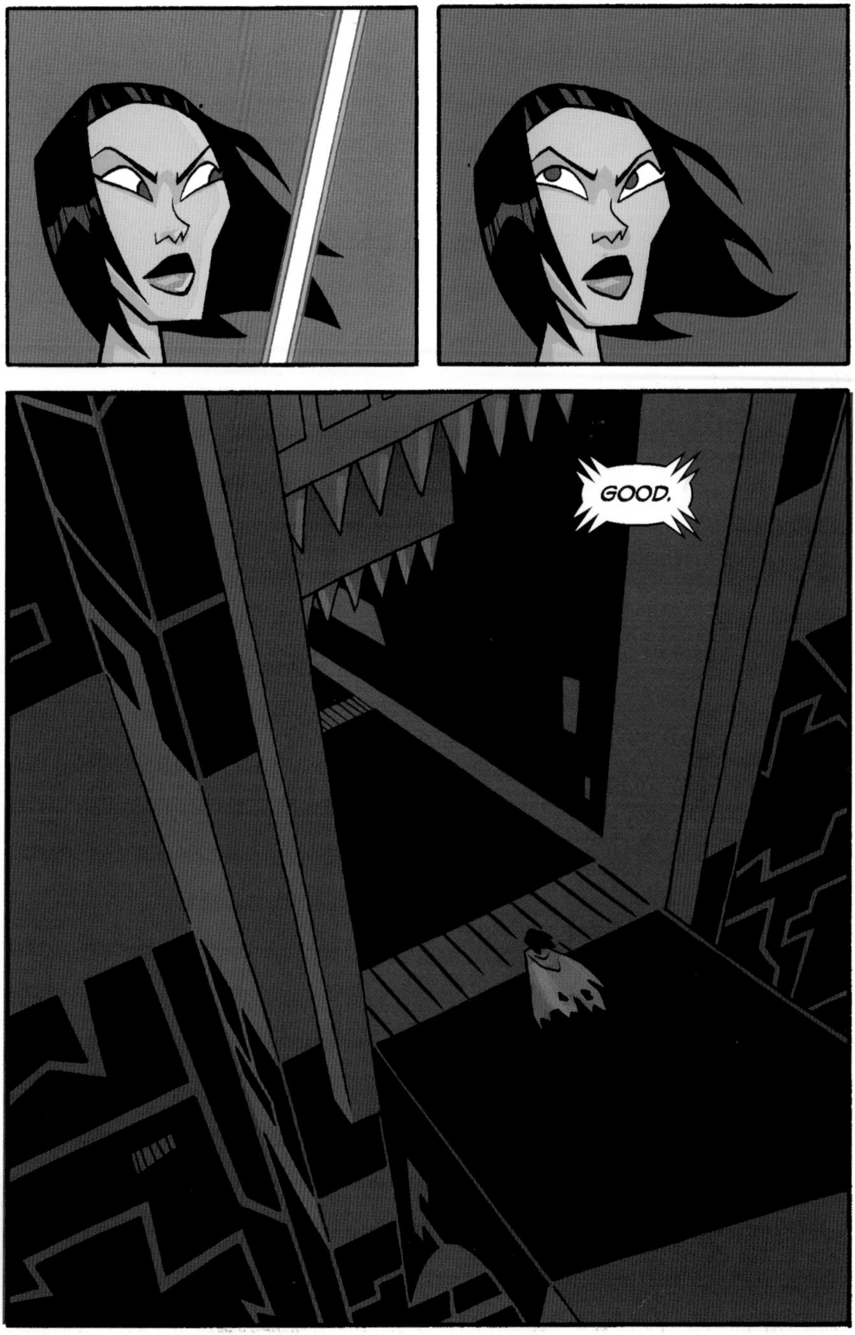
GOOD.

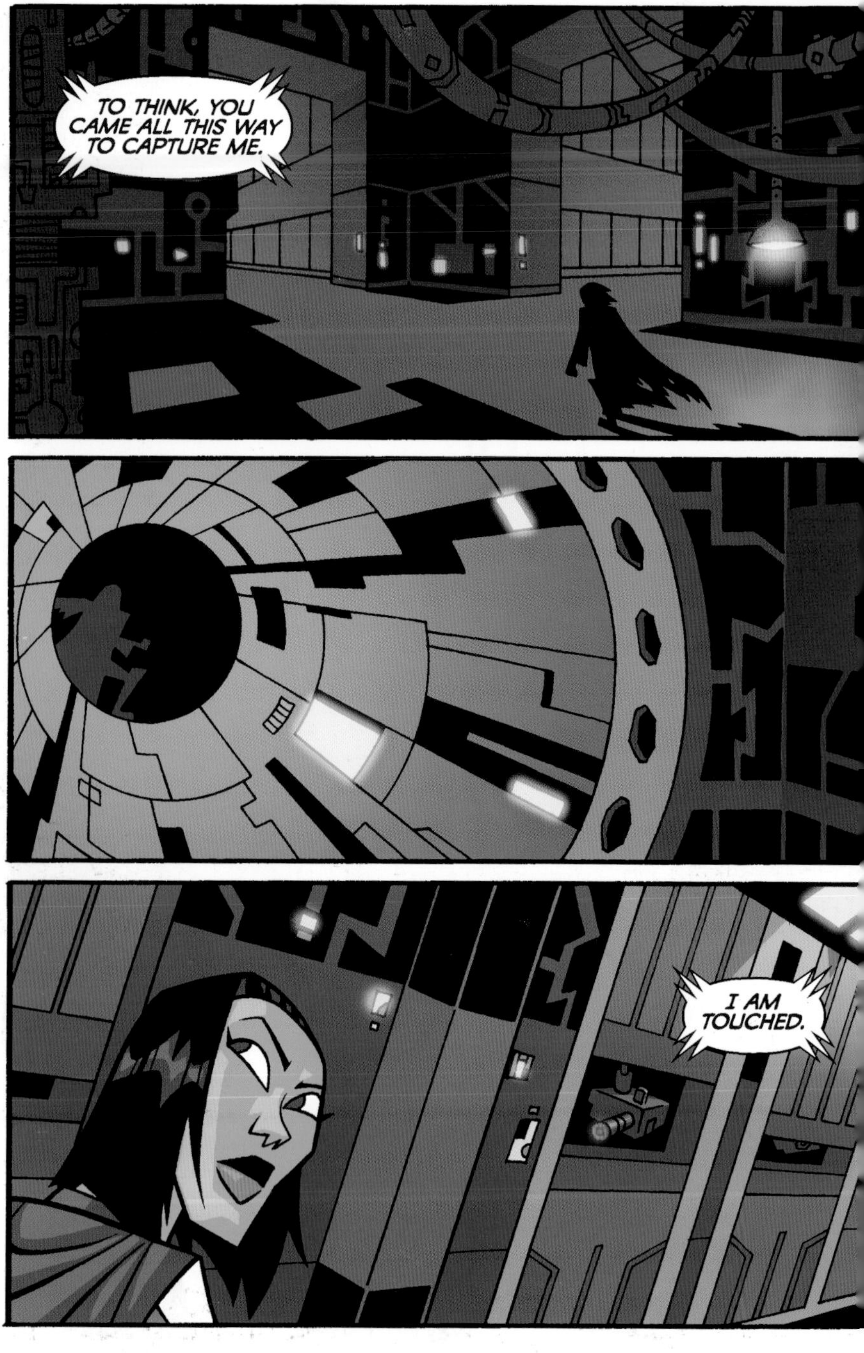
TO THINK, YOU CAME ALL THIS WAY TO CAPTURE ME.
I AM TOUCHED.

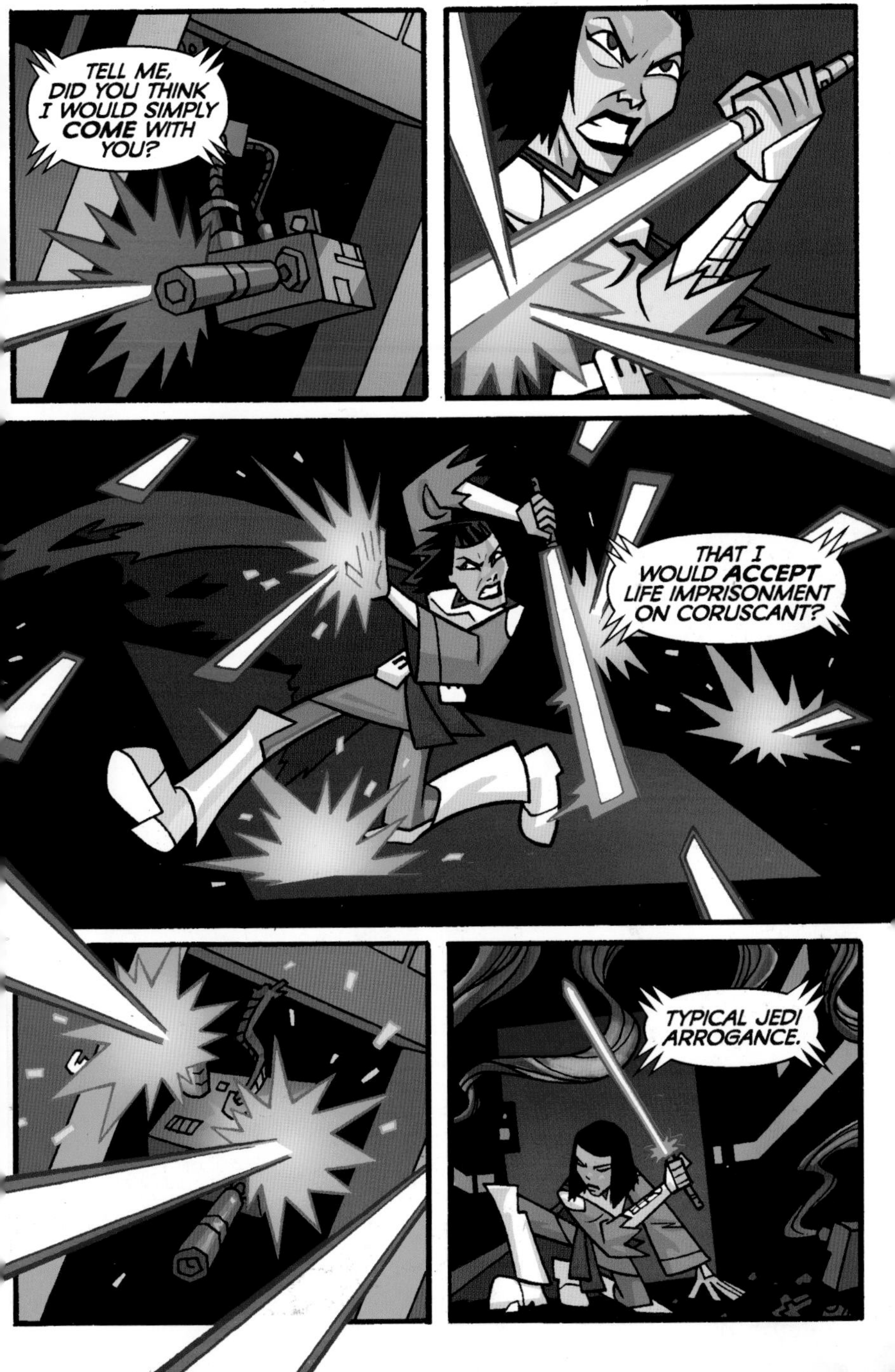
TELL ME, DID YOU THINK I WOULD SIMPLY COME WITH YOU?
THAT I WOULD ACCEPT LIFE IMPRISONMENT ON CORUSCANT?
TYPICAL JEDI ARROGANCE.

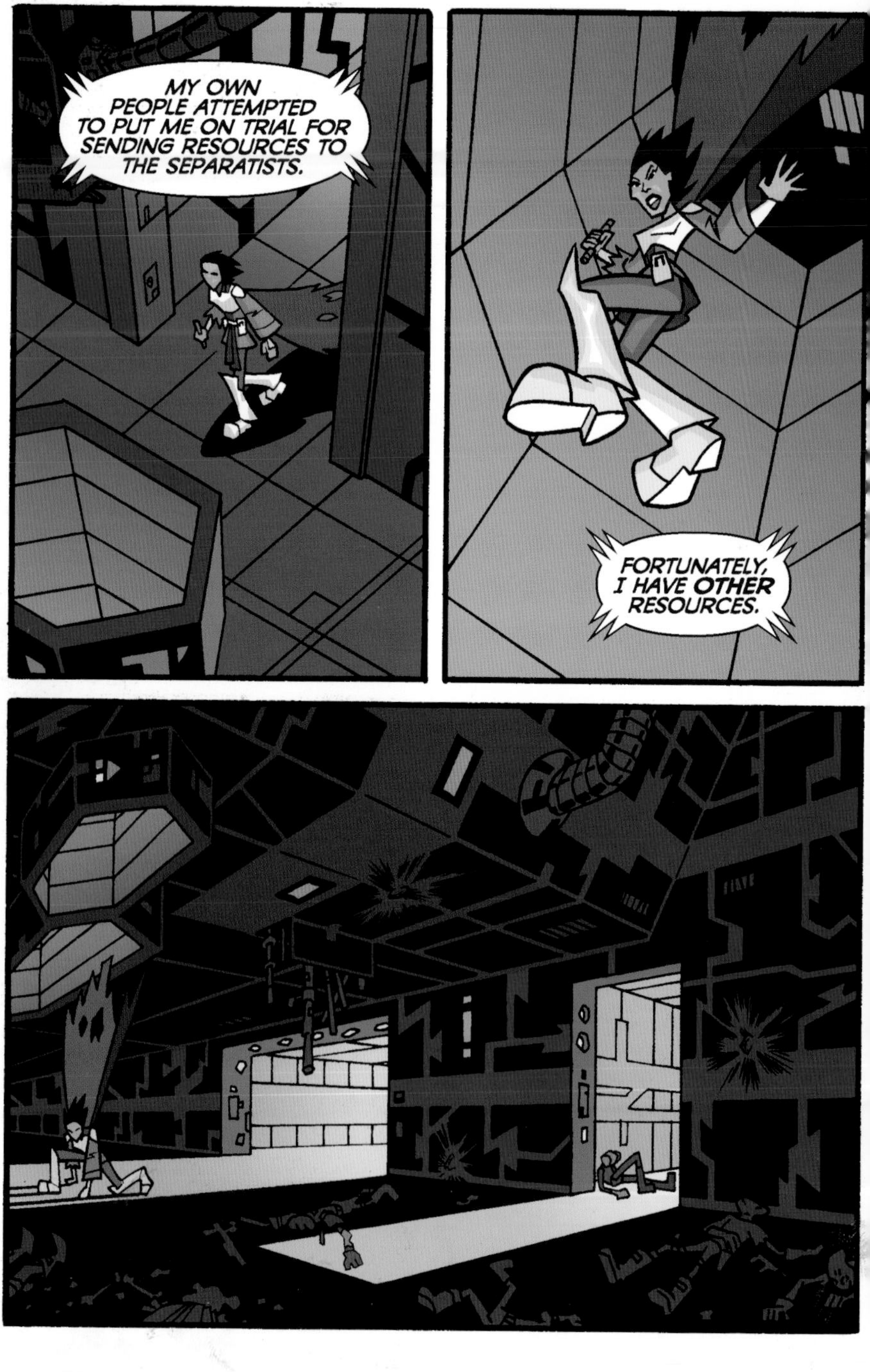
MY OWN PEOPLE ATTEMPTED TO PUT ME ON TRIAL FOR SENDING RESOURCES TO THE SEPARATISTS.
FORTUNATELY, I HAVE OTHER RESOURCES.

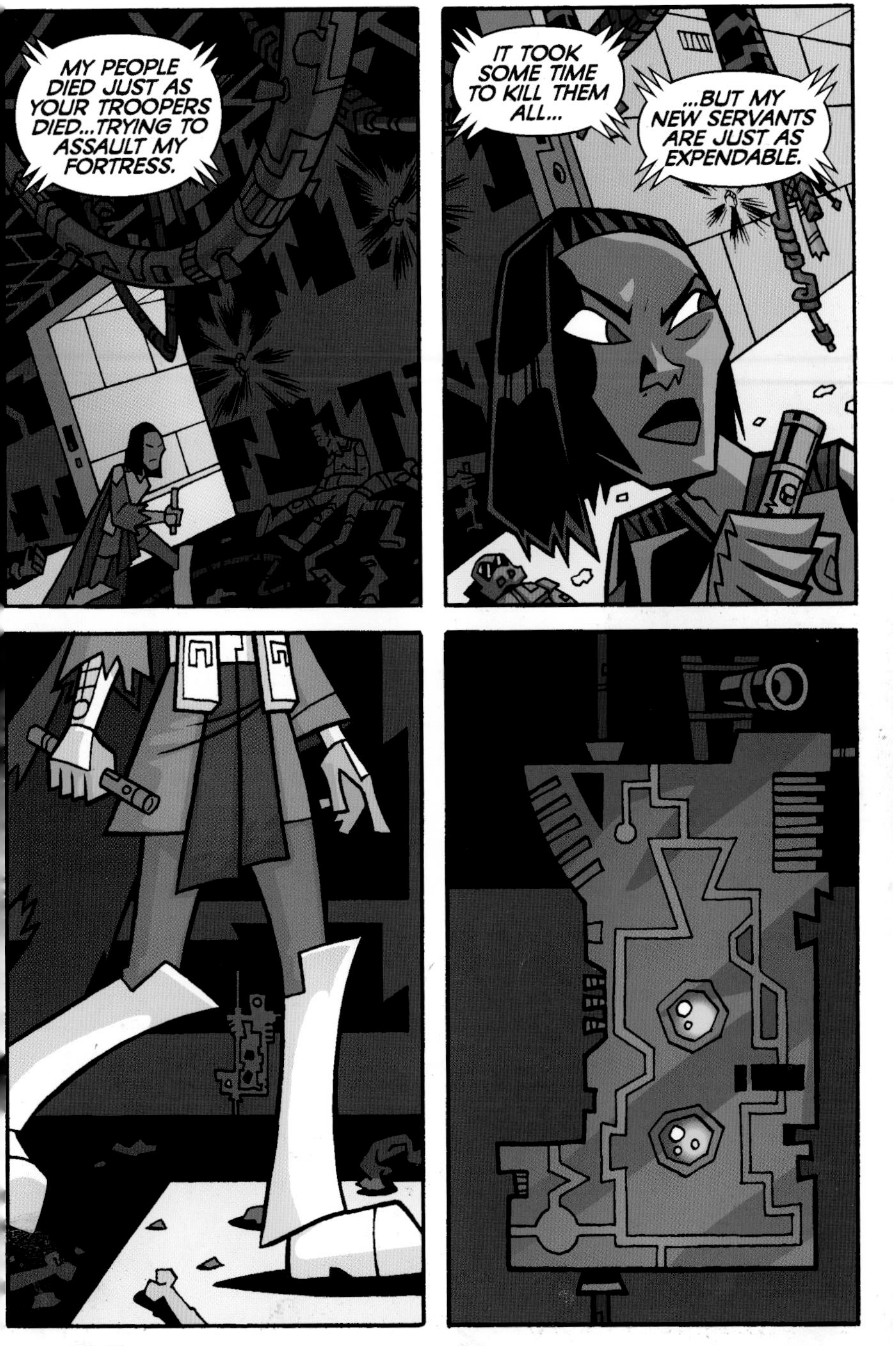
MY PEOPLE DIED JUST AS YOUR TROOPERS DIED...TRYING TO ASSAULT MY FORTRESS.
IT TOOK SOME TIME TO KILL THEM ALL...
...BUT MY NEW SERVANTS ARE JUST AS EXPENDABLE.

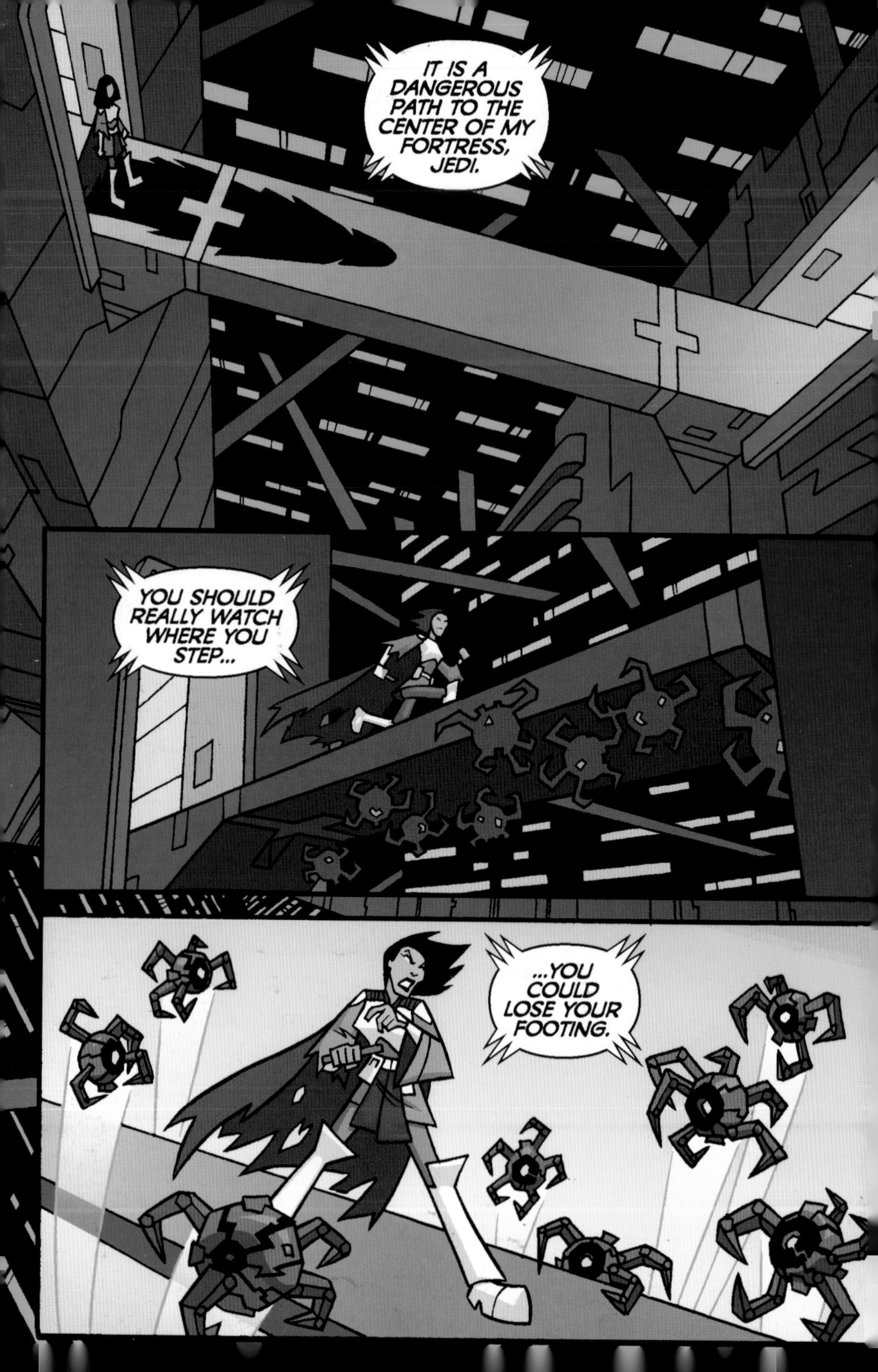
IT IS A DANGEROUS PATH TO THE CENTER OF MY FORTRESS, JEDI.
YOU SHOULD REALLY WATCH WHERE YOU STEP...
...YOU COULD LOSE YOUR FOOTING.

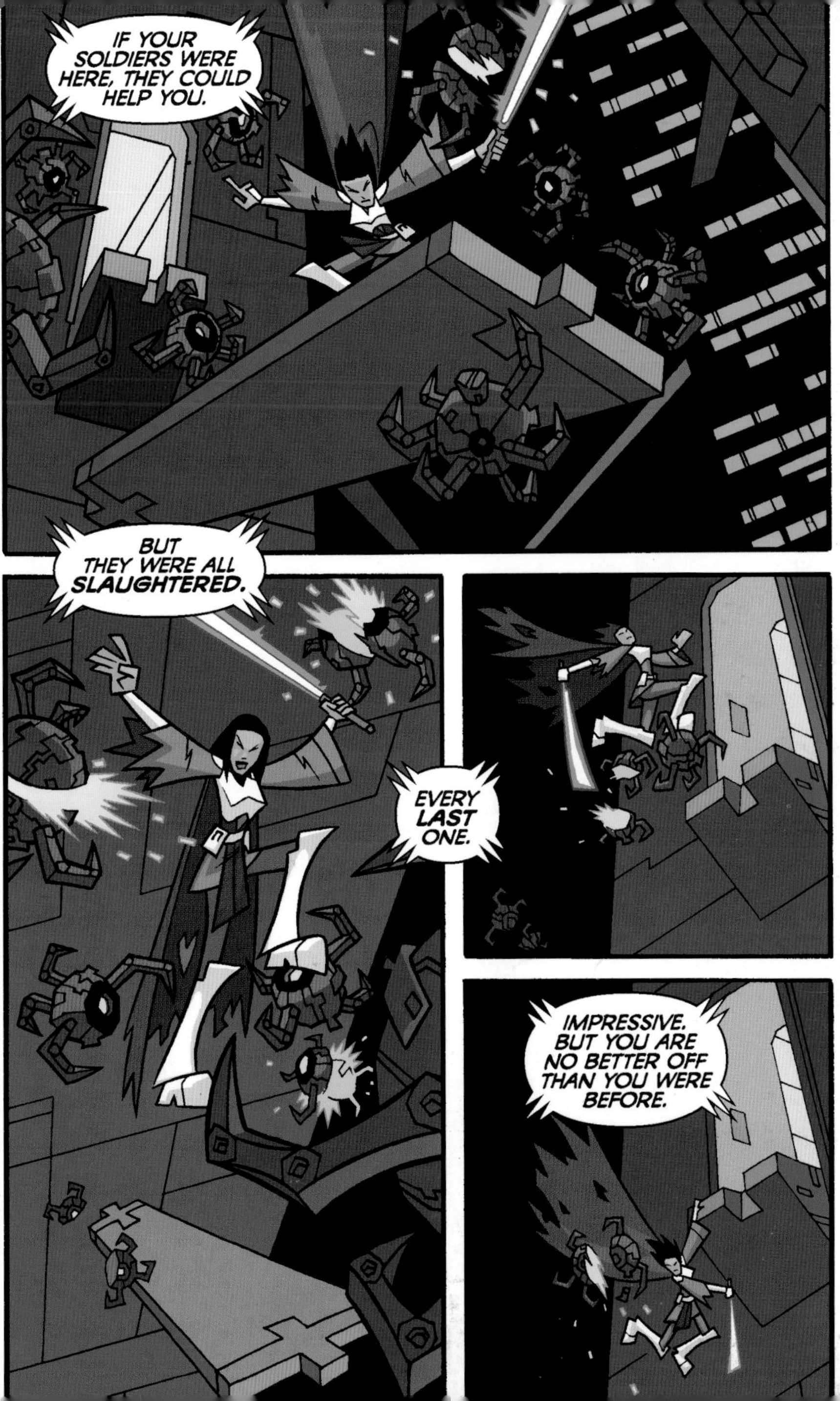
IF YOUR SOLDIERS WERE HERE, THEY COULD HELP YOU.
BUT THEY WERE ALL SLAUGHTERED.
EVERY LAST ONE.
IMPRESSIVE. BUT YOU ARE NO BETTER OFF THAN YOU WERE BEFORE.

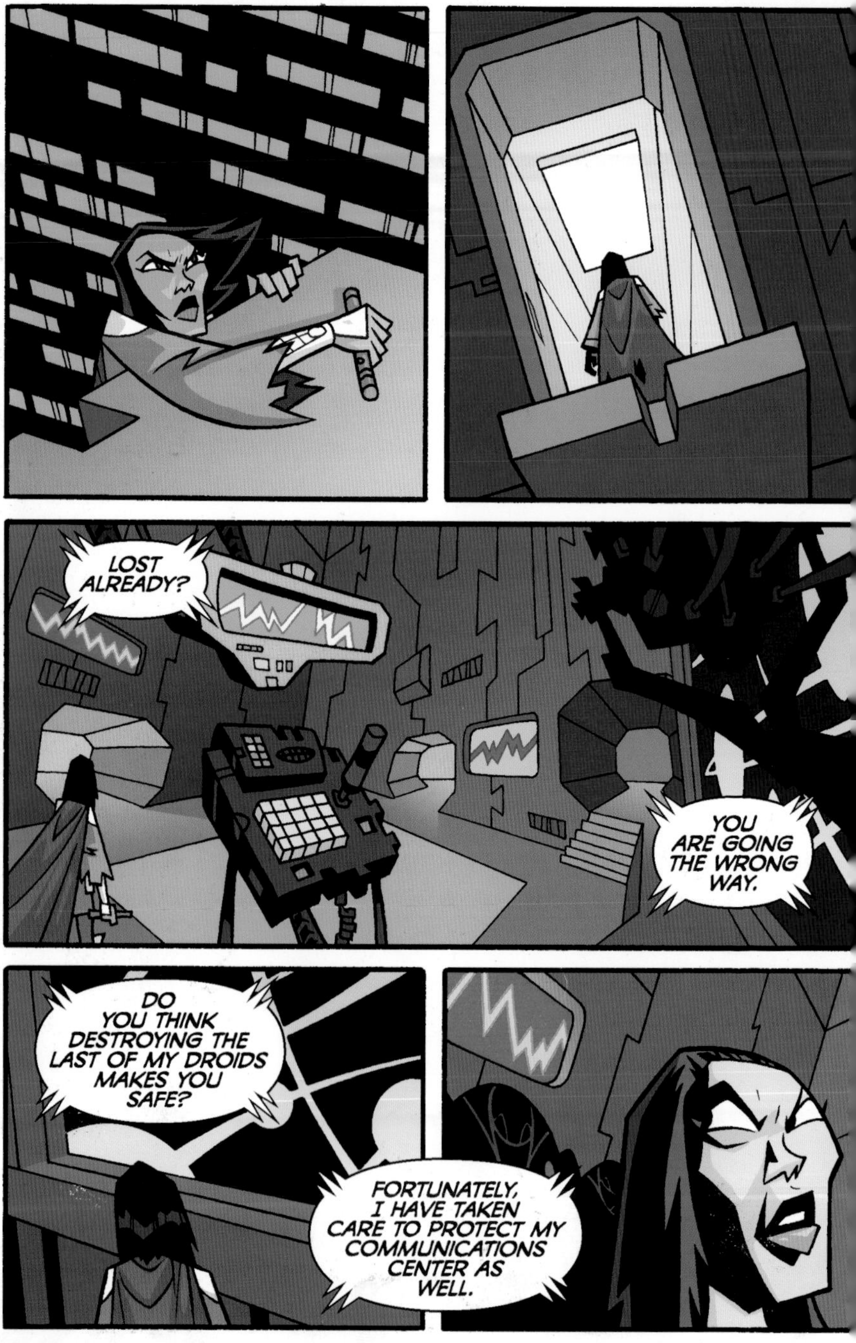
LOST ALREADY?
YOU ARE GOING THE WRONG WAY.
DO YOU THINK DESTROYING THE LAST OF MY DROIDS MAKES YOU SAFE?
FORTUNATELY, I HAVE TAKEN CARE TO PROTECT MY COMMUNICATIONS CENTER AS WELL.

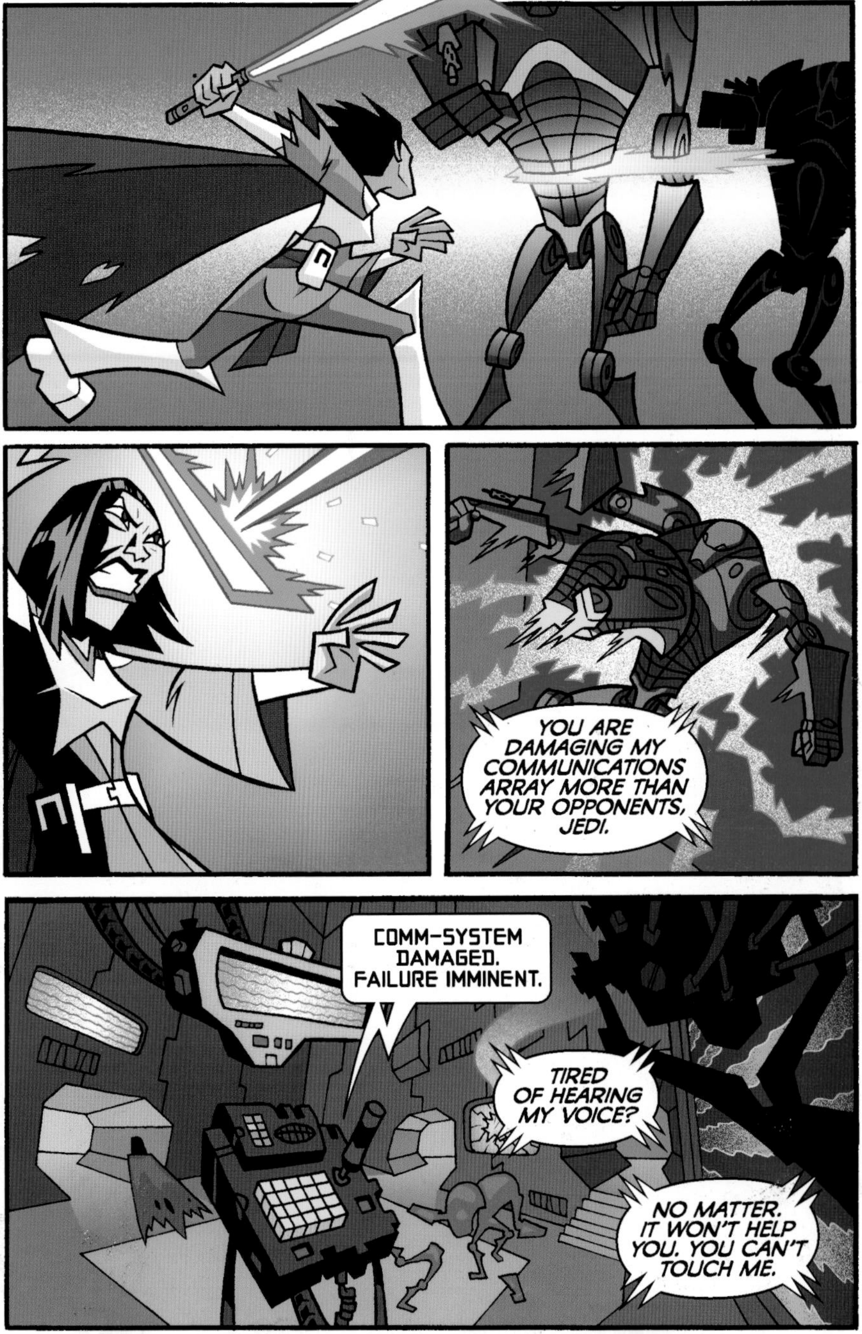
YOU ARE DAMAGING MY COMMUNICATIONS ARRAY MORE THAN YOUR OPPONENTS, JEDI.
COMM-SYSTEM DAMAGED. FAILURE IMMINENT.
TIRED OF HEARING MY VOICE?
NO MATTER. IT WON'T HELP YOU. YOU CAN'T TOUCH ME.

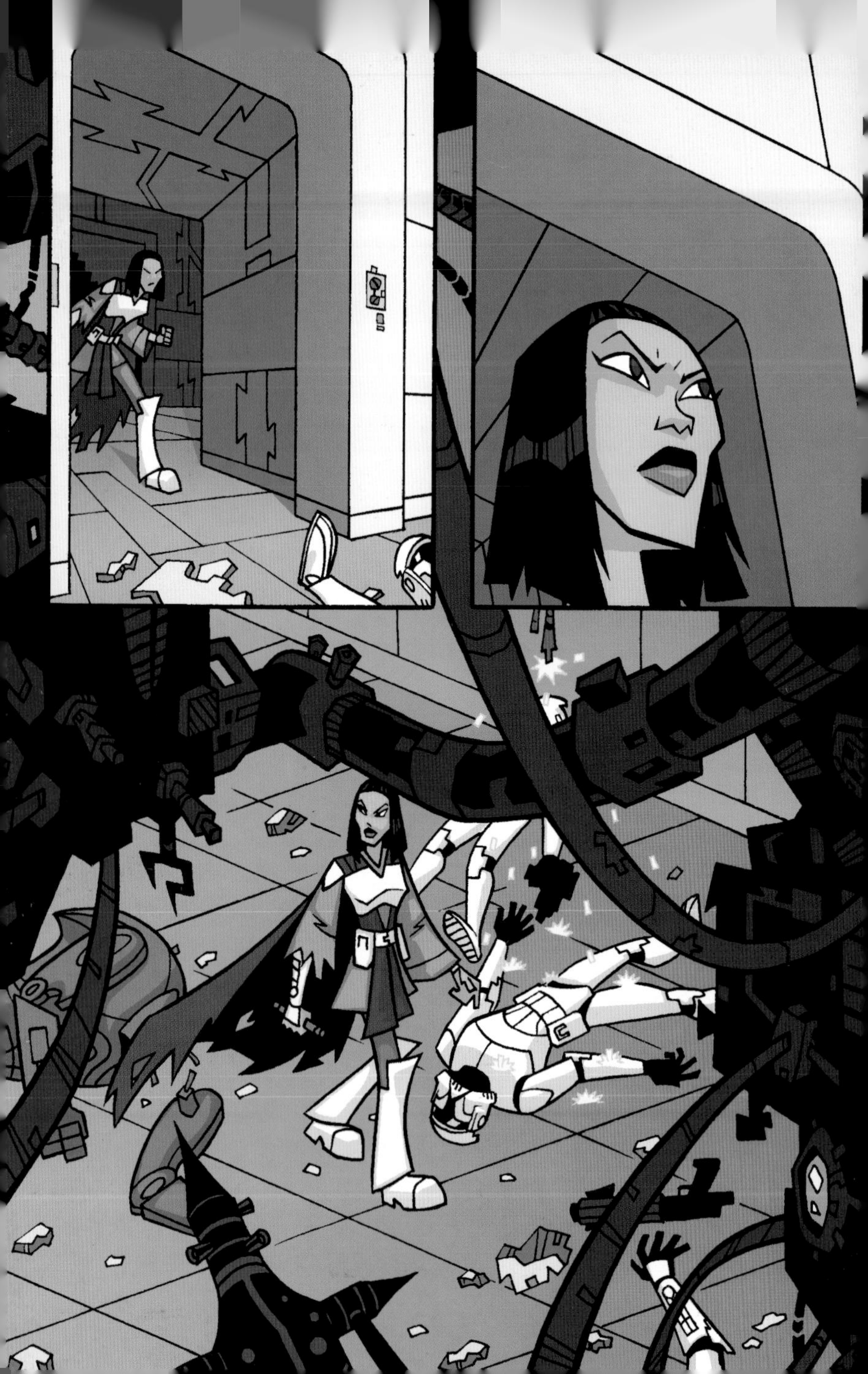

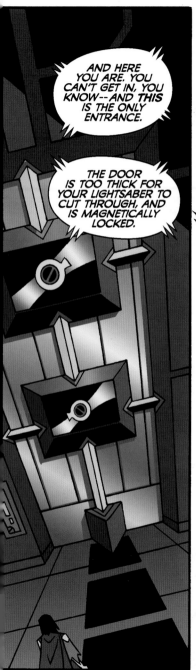

AND HERE YOU ARE. YOU CAN'T GET IN, YOU KNOW-- AND *THIS* IS THE ONLY ENTRANCE.

THE DOOR IS TOO THICK FOR YOUR LIGHTSABER TO CUT THROUGH, AND IS MAGNETICALLY LOCKED.

VVMMMM!!

THE MECHANISM IS TRIPLE-CODED AND...

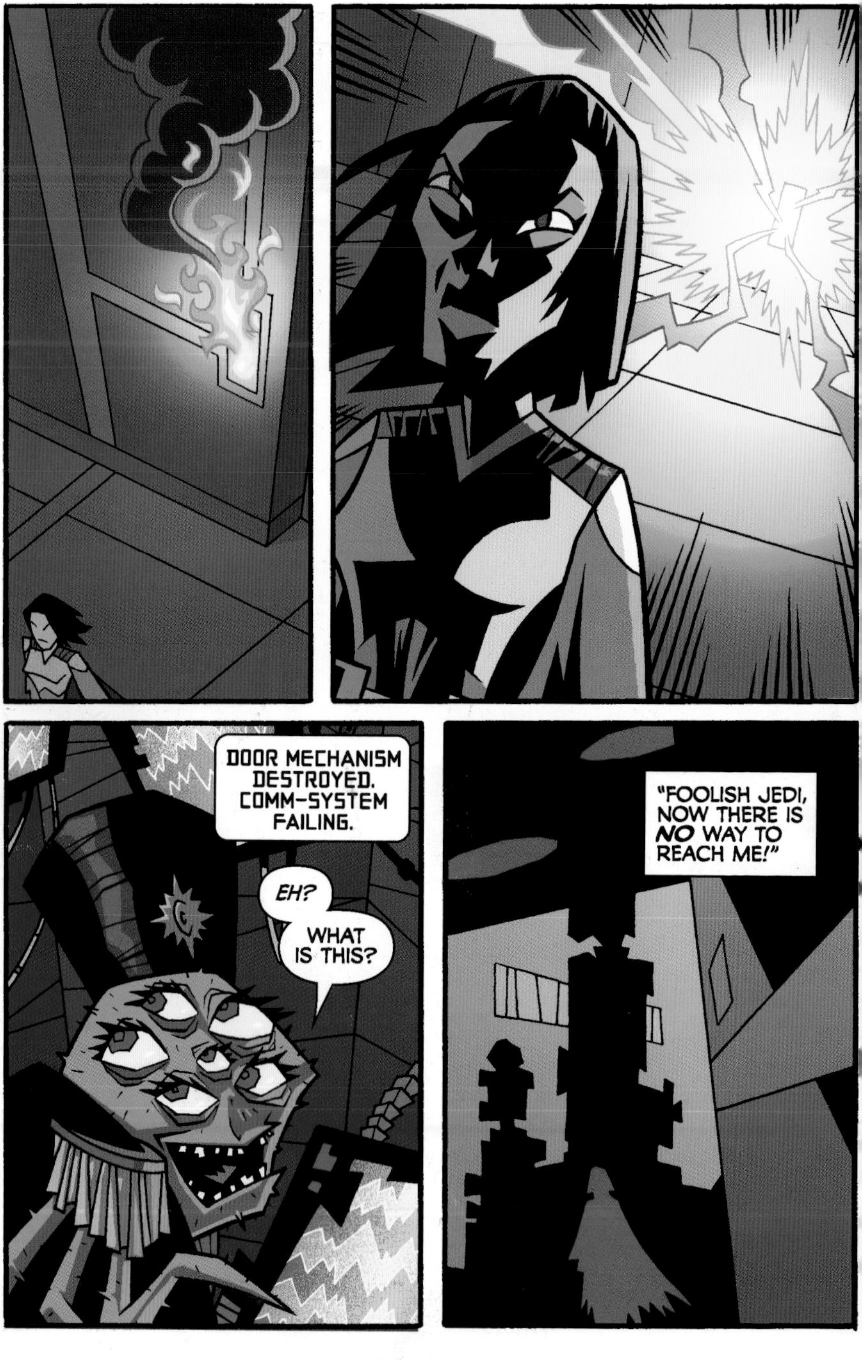
DOOR MECHANISM DESTROYED. COMM-SYSTEM FAILING.
EH?
WHAT IS THIS?
"FOOLISH JEDI, NOW THERE IS NO WAY TO REACH ME!"

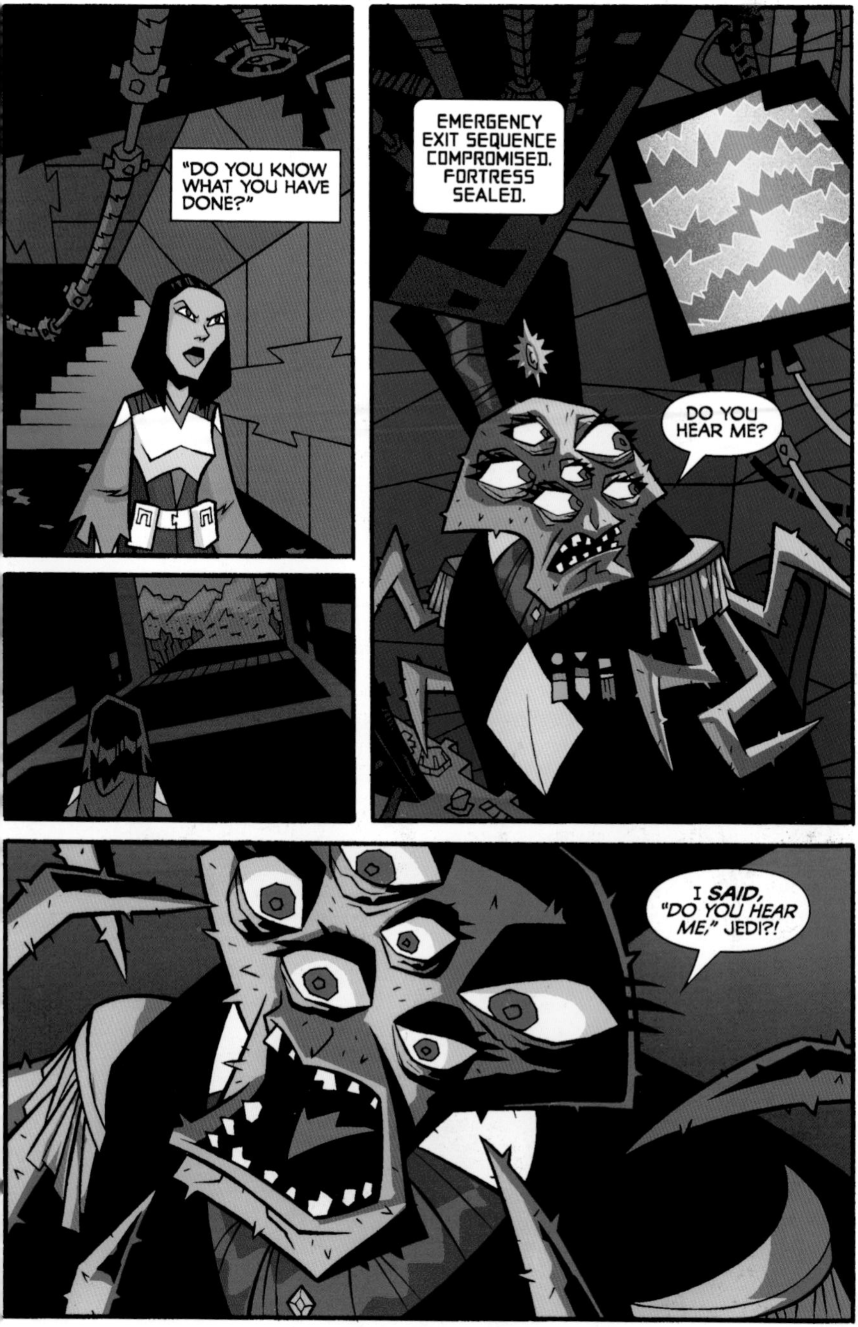
"DO YOU KNOW WHAT YOU HAVE DONE?"
EMERGENCY EXIT SEQUENCE COMPROMISED. FORTRESS SEALED.
DO YOU HEAR ME?
I *SAID,* "DO YOU HEAR *ME,*" JEDI?!

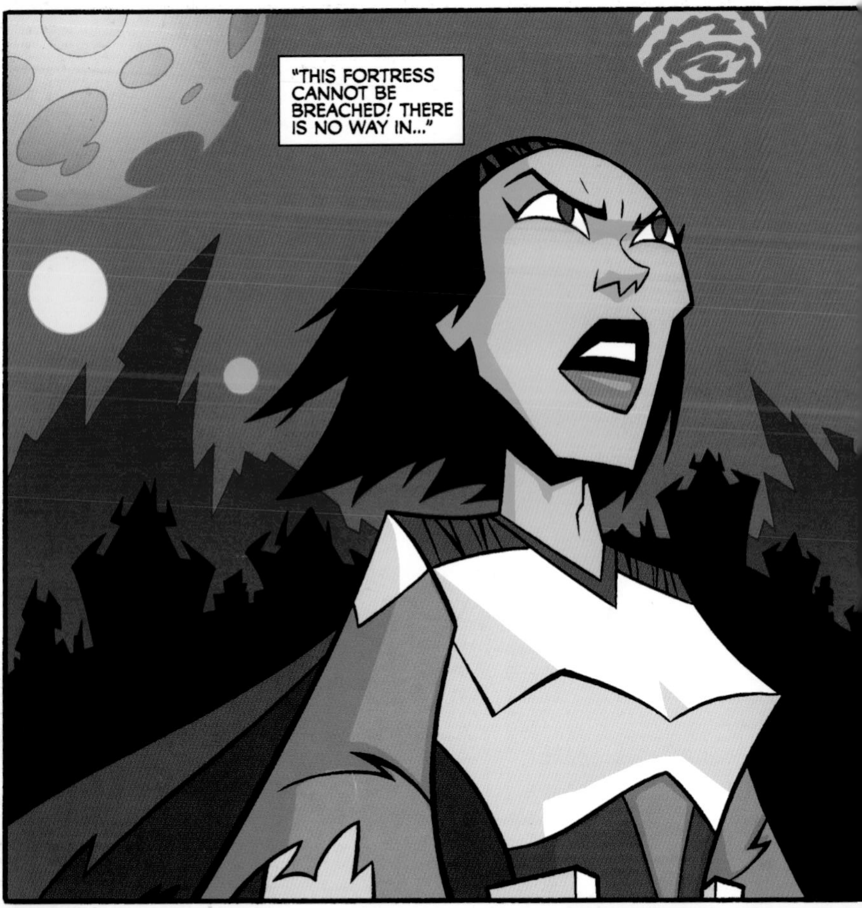
"THIS FORTRESS CANNOT BE BREACHED! THERE IS NO WAY IN..."
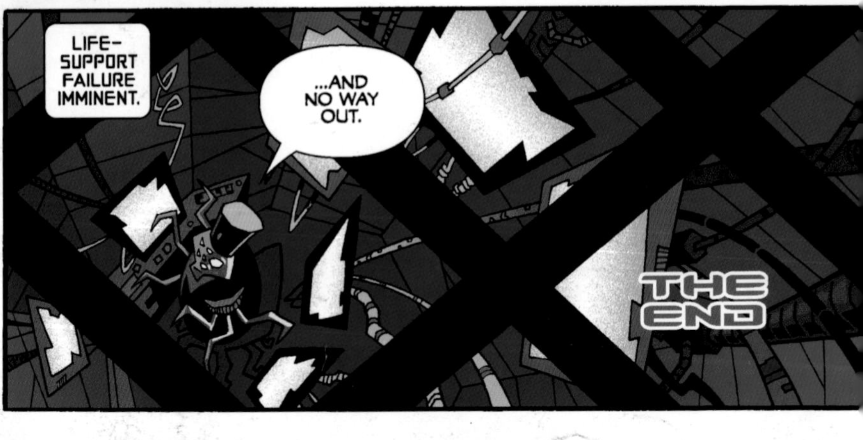
LIFE-SUPPORT FAILURE IMMINENT.
...AND NO WAY OUT.
THE END

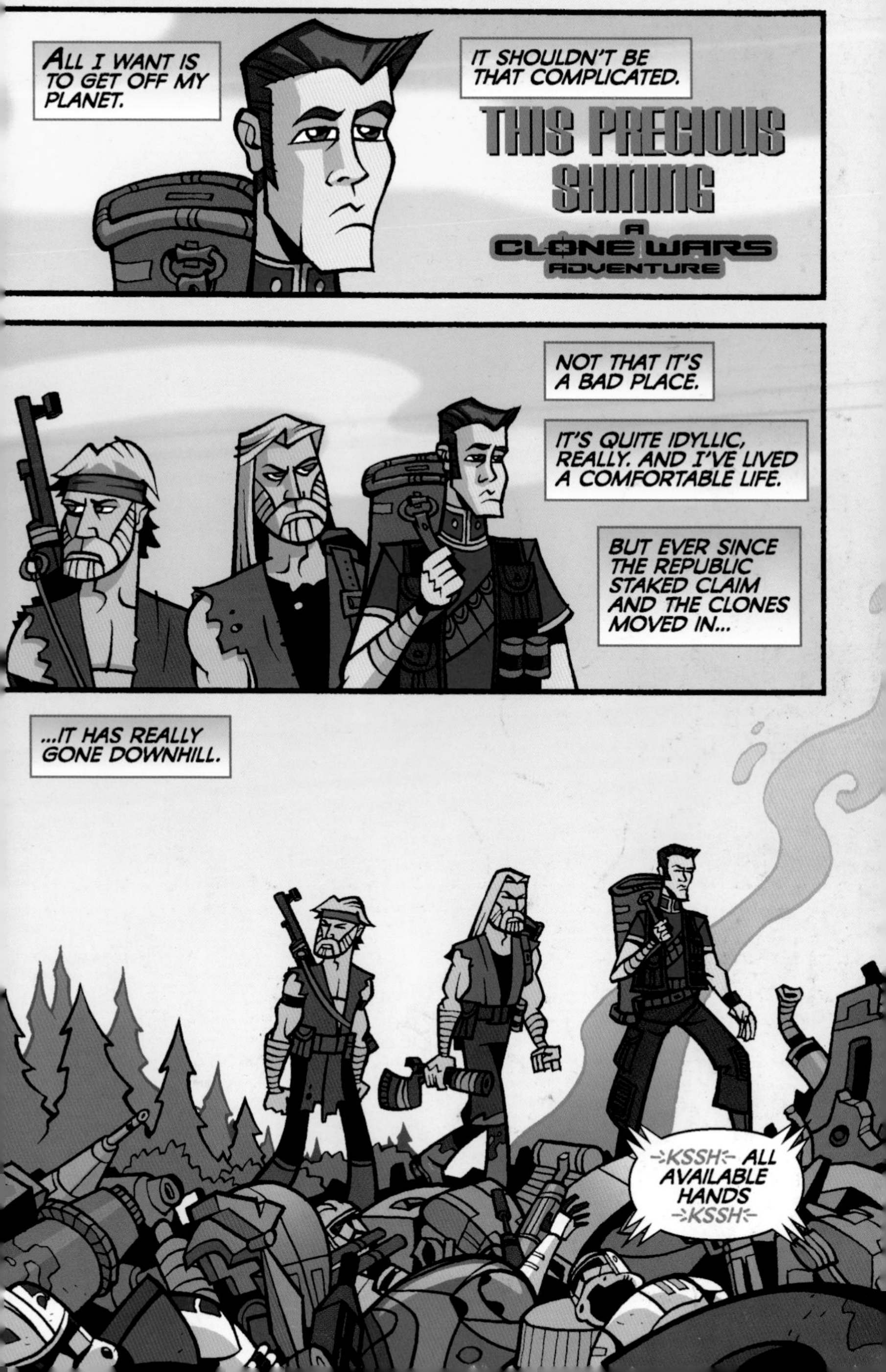
ALL I WANT IS TO GET OFF MY PLANET.
IT SHOULDN'T BE THAT COMPLICATED.
THIS PRECIOUS SHINING
A CLONE WARS ADVENTURE
NOT THAT IT'S A BAD PLACE.
IT'S QUITE IDYLLIC, REALLY. AND I'VE LIVED A COMFORTABLE LIFE.
BUT EVER SINCE THE REPUBLIC STAKED CLAIM AND THE CLONES MOVED IN...
...IT HAS REALLY GONE DOWNHILL.
-KSSH- ALL AVAILABLE HANDS -KSSH-

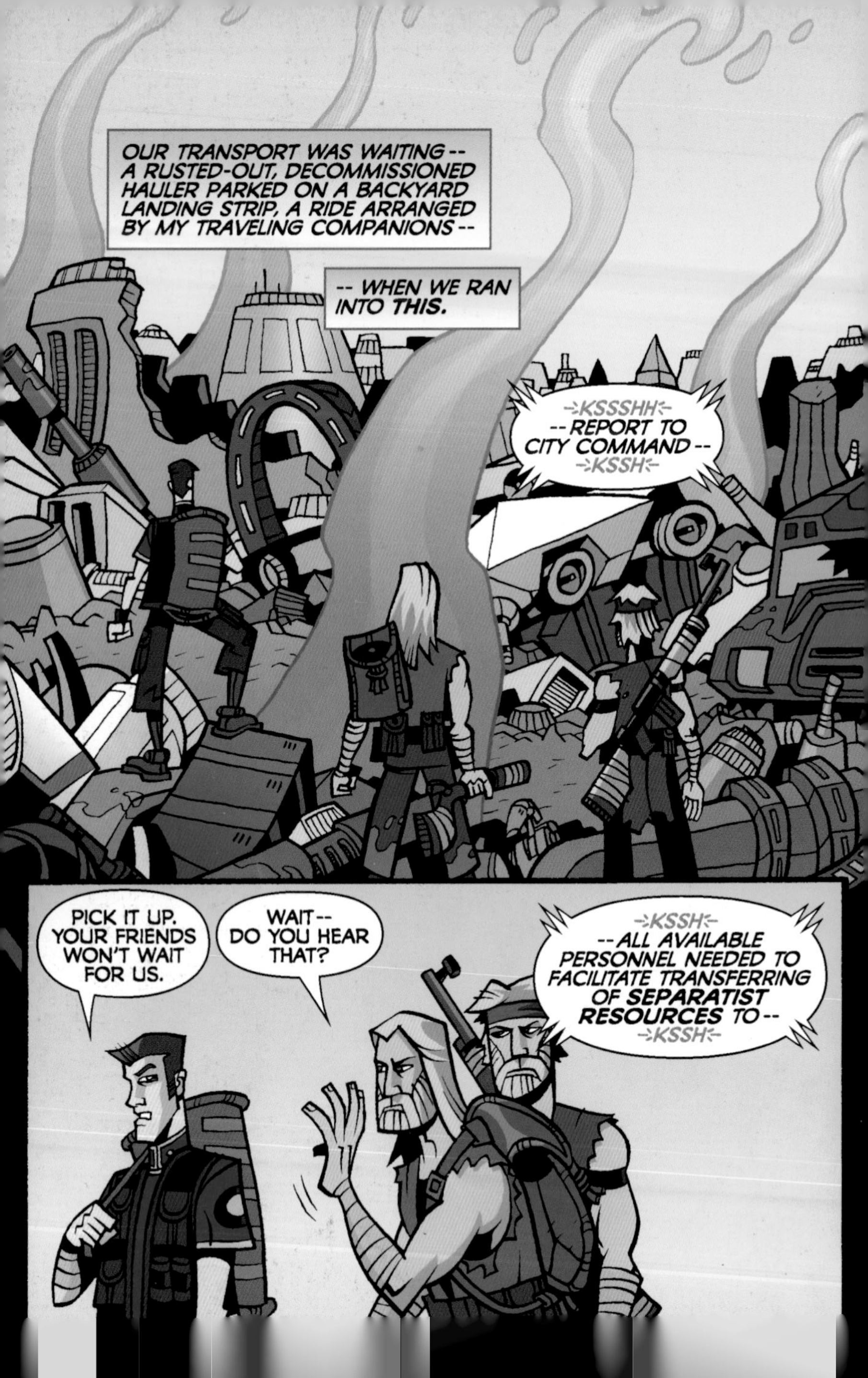
OUR TRANSPORT WAS WAITING -- A RUSTED-OUT, DECOMMISSIONED HAULER PARKED ON A BACKYARD LANDING STRIP, A RIDE ARRANGED BY MY TRAVELING COMPANIONS --
-- WHEN WE RAN INTO THIS.
KSSSHH -- REPORT TO CITY COMMAND -- KSSH
PICK IT UP. YOUR FRIENDS WON'T WAIT FOR US.
WAIT -- DO YOU HEAR THAT?
KSSH -- ALL AVAILABLE PERSONNEL NEEDED TO FACILITATE TRANSFERRING OF SEPARATIST RESOURCES TO -- KSSH

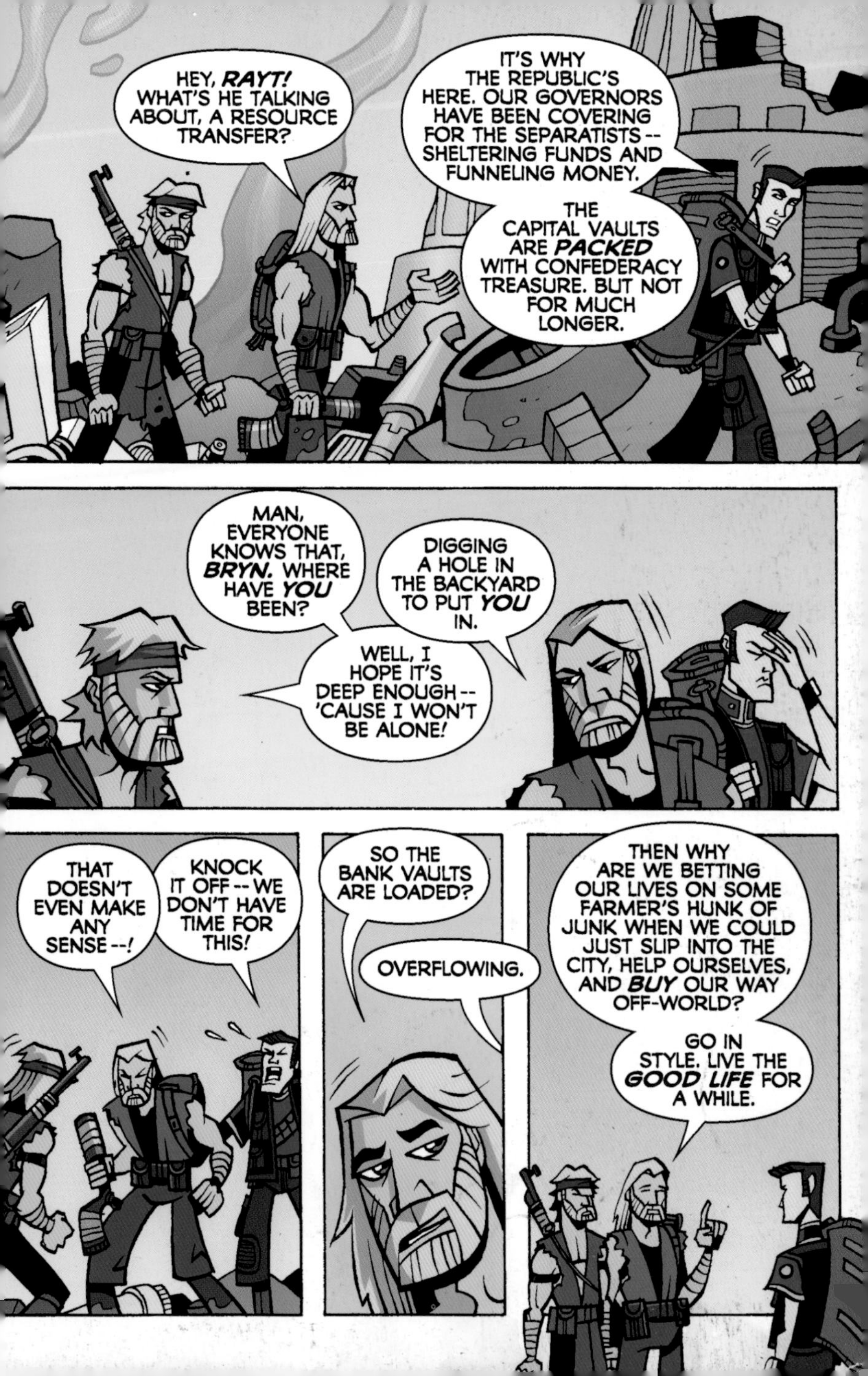
HEY, RAYT! WHAT'S HE TALKING ABOUT, A RESOURCE TRANSFER?
IT'S WHY THE REPUBLIC'S HERE. OUR GOVERNORS HAVE BEEN COVERING FOR THE SEPARATISTS -- SHELTERING FUNDS AND FUNNELING MONEY.
THE CAPITAL VAULTS ARE PACKED WITH CONFEDERACY TREASURE. BUT NOT FOR MUCH LONGER.
MAN, EVERYONE KNOWS THAT, BRYN. WHERE HAVE YOU BEEN?
DIGGING A HOLE IN THE BACKYARD TO PUT YOU IN.
WELL, I HOPE IT'S DEEP ENOUGH -- 'CAUSE I WON'T BE ALONE!
THAT DOESN'T EVEN MAKE ANY SENSE --!
KNOCK IT OFF -- WE DON'T HAVE TIME FOR THIS!
SO THE BANK VAULTS ARE LOADED?
OVERFLOWING.
THEN WHY ARE WE BETTING OUR LIVES ON SOME FARMER'S HUNK OF JUNK WHEN WE COULD JUST SLIP INTO THE CITY, HELP OURSELVES, AND BUY OUR WAY OFF-WORLD?
GO IN STYLE. LIVE THE GOOD LIFE FOR A WHILE.

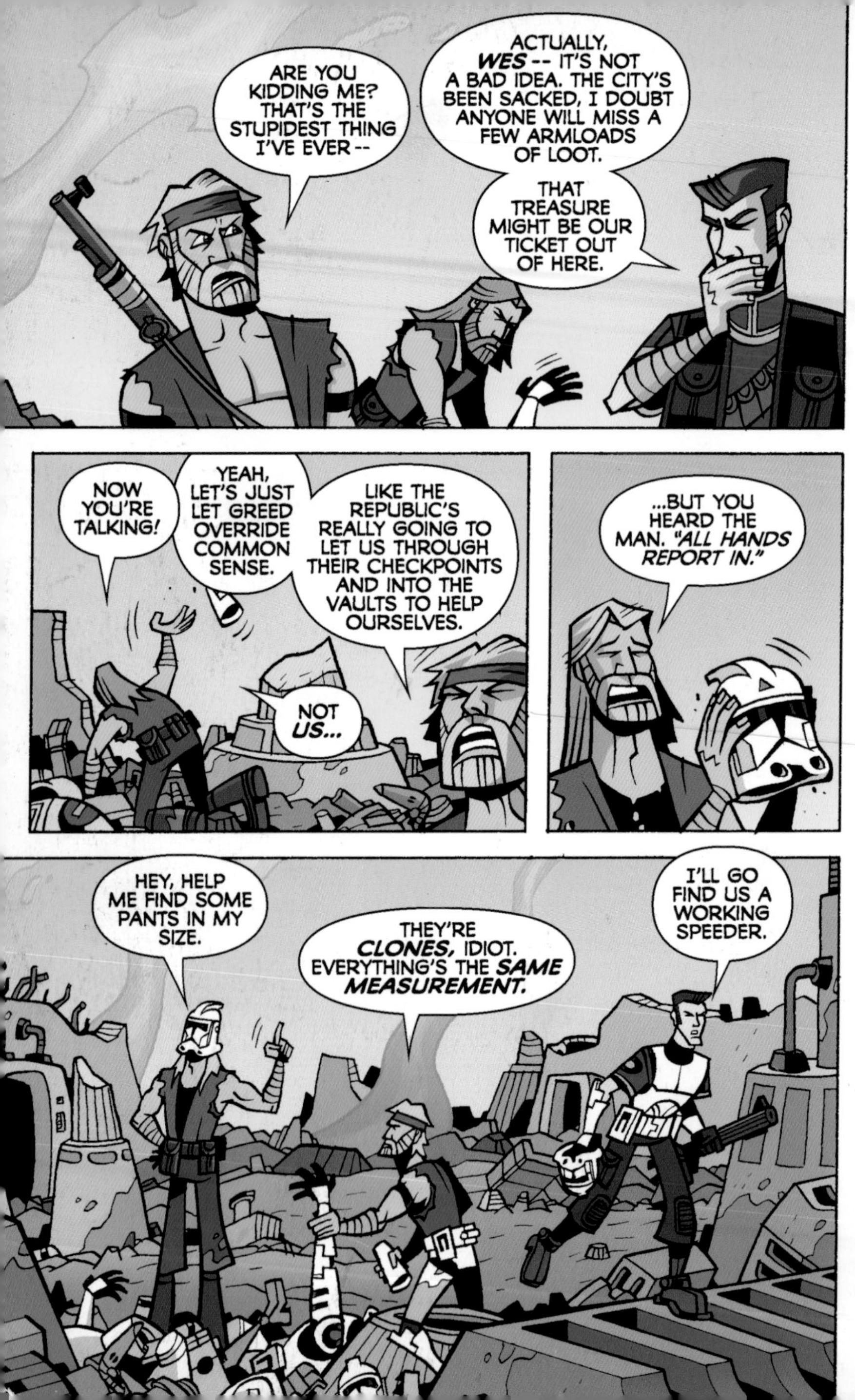
ARE YOU KIDDING ME? THAT'S THE STUPIDEST THING I'VE EVER --
ACTUALLY, WES -- IT'S NOT A BAD IDEA. THE CITY'S BEEN SACKED, I DOUBT ANYONE WILL MISS A FEW ARMLOADS OF LOOT.
THAT TREASURE MIGHT BE OUR TICKET OUT OF HERE.
NOW YOU'RE TALKING!
YEAH, LET'S JUST LET GREED OVERRIDE COMMON SENSE.
LIKE THE REPUBLIC'S REALLY GOING TO LET US THROUGH THEIR CHECKPOINTS AND INTO THE VAULTS TO HELP OURSELVES.
NOT US...
...BUT YOU HEARD THE MAN. "ALL HANDS REPORT IN."
HEY, HELP ME FIND SOME PANTS IN MY SIZE.
THEY'RE CLONES, IDIOT. EVERYTHING'S THE SAME MEASUREMENT.
I'LL GO FIND US A WORKING SPEEDER.

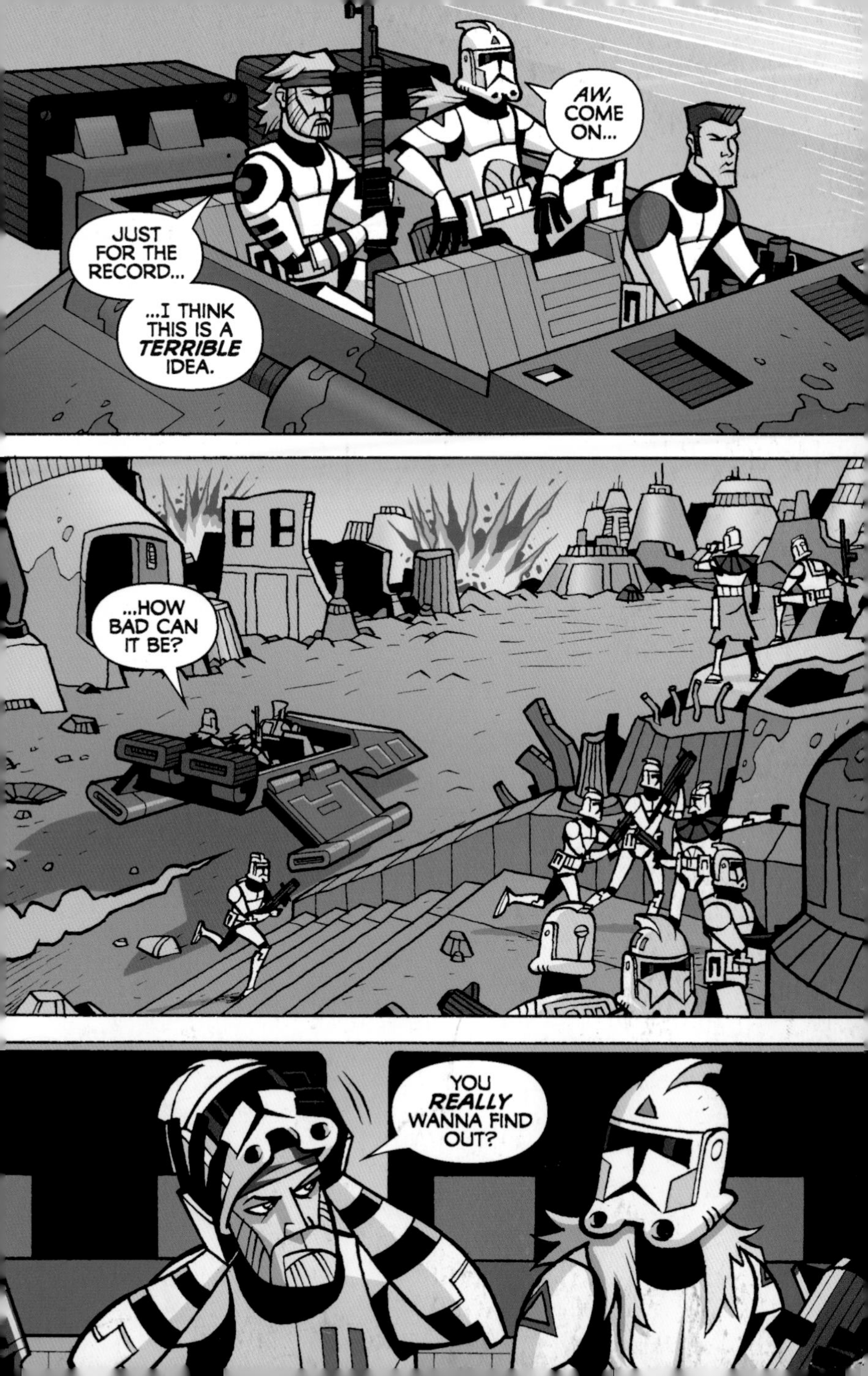
AW, COME ON...
JUST FOR THE RECORD...
...I THINK THIS IS A TERRIBLE IDEA.
...HOW BAD CAN IT BE?
YOU REALLY WANNA FIND OUT?

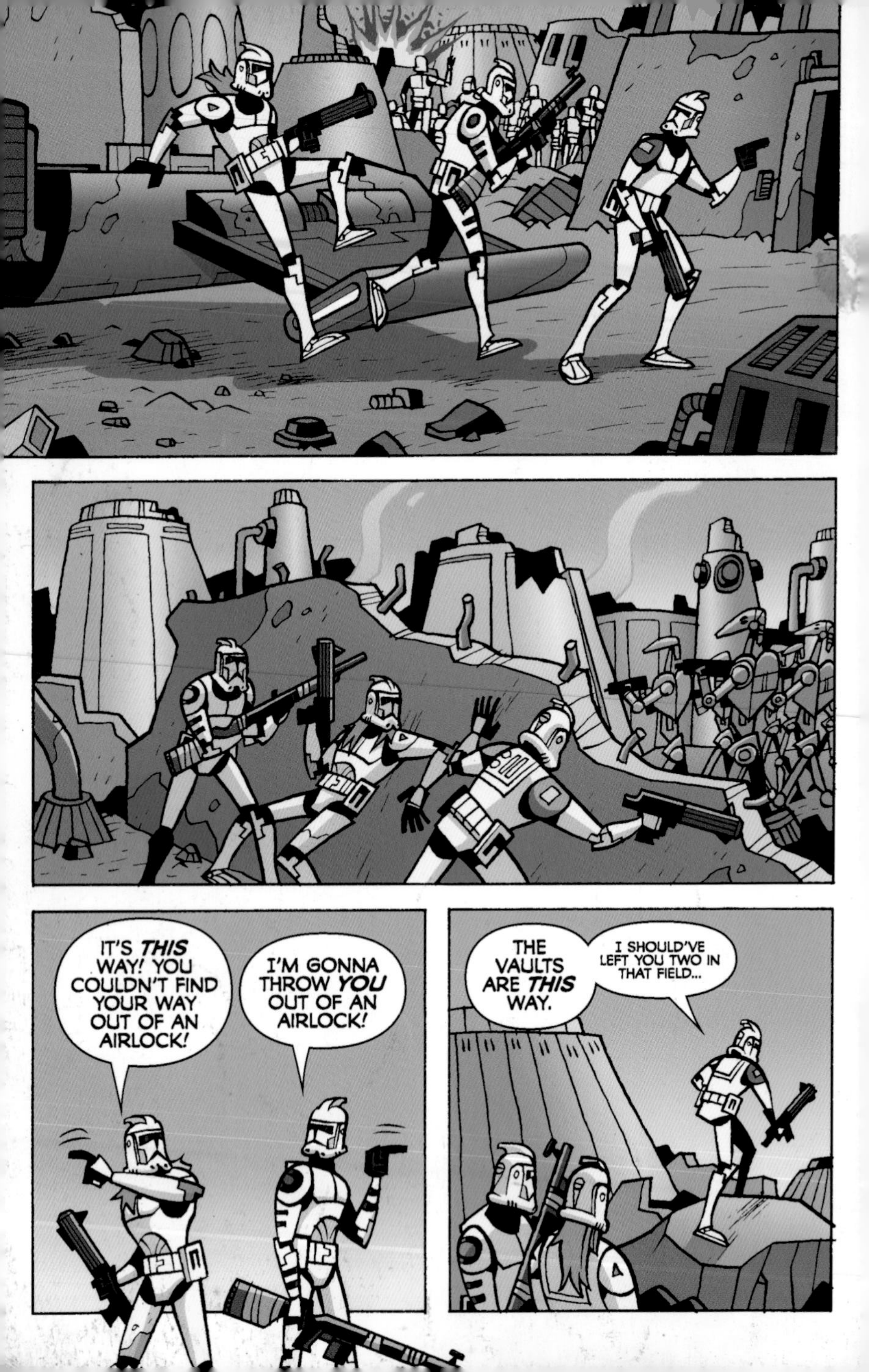
IT'S *THIS* WAY! YOU COULDN'T FIND YOUR WAY OUT OF AN AIRLOCK!
I'M GONNA THROW *YOU* OUT OF AN AIRLOCK!
THE VAULTS ARE *THIS* WAY.
I SHOULD'VE LEFT YOU TWO IN THAT FIELD...

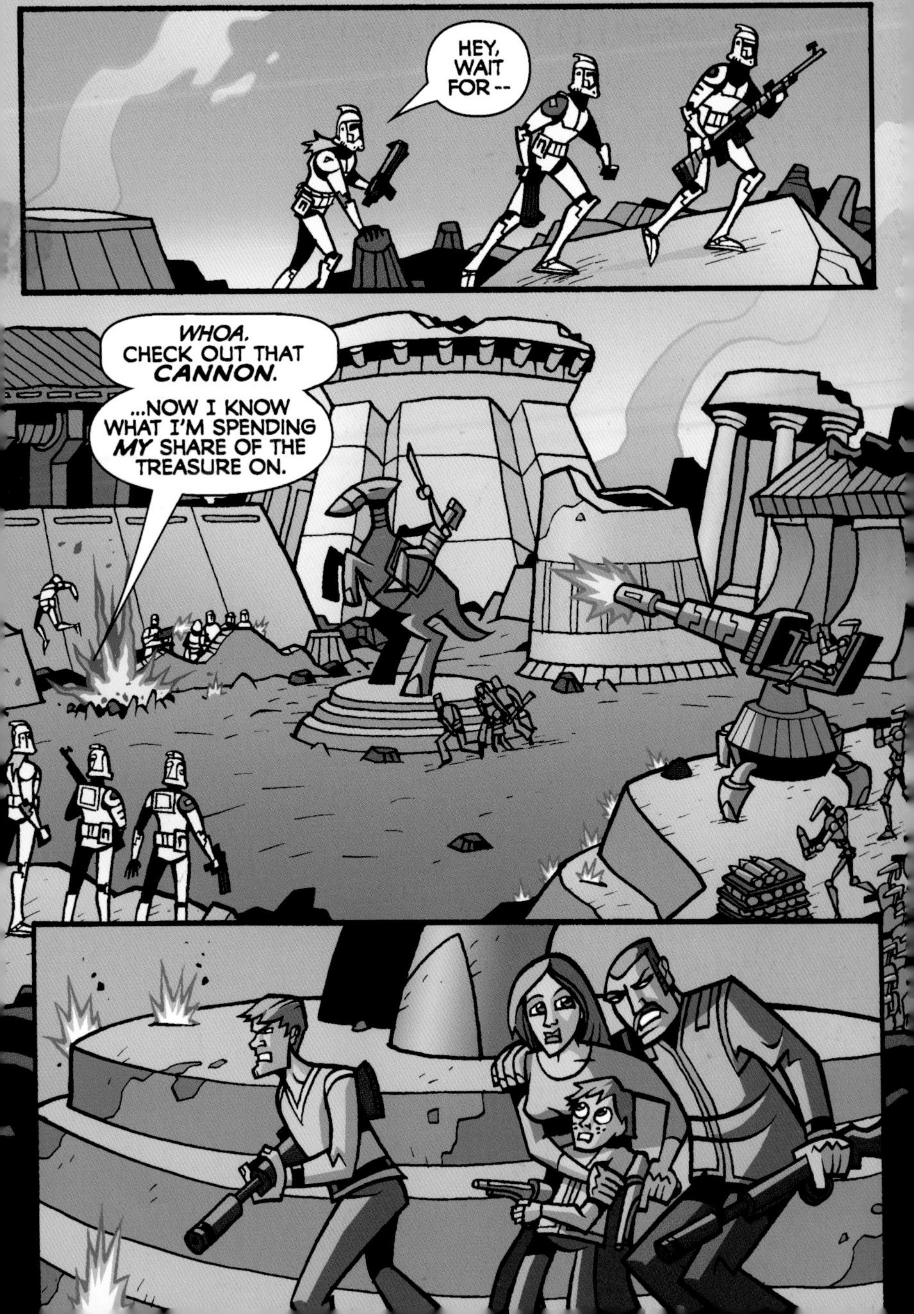
HEY, WAIT FOR--
WHOA. CHECK OUT THAT CANNON.
...NOW I KNOW WHAT I'M SPENDING MY SHARE OF THE TREASURE ON.

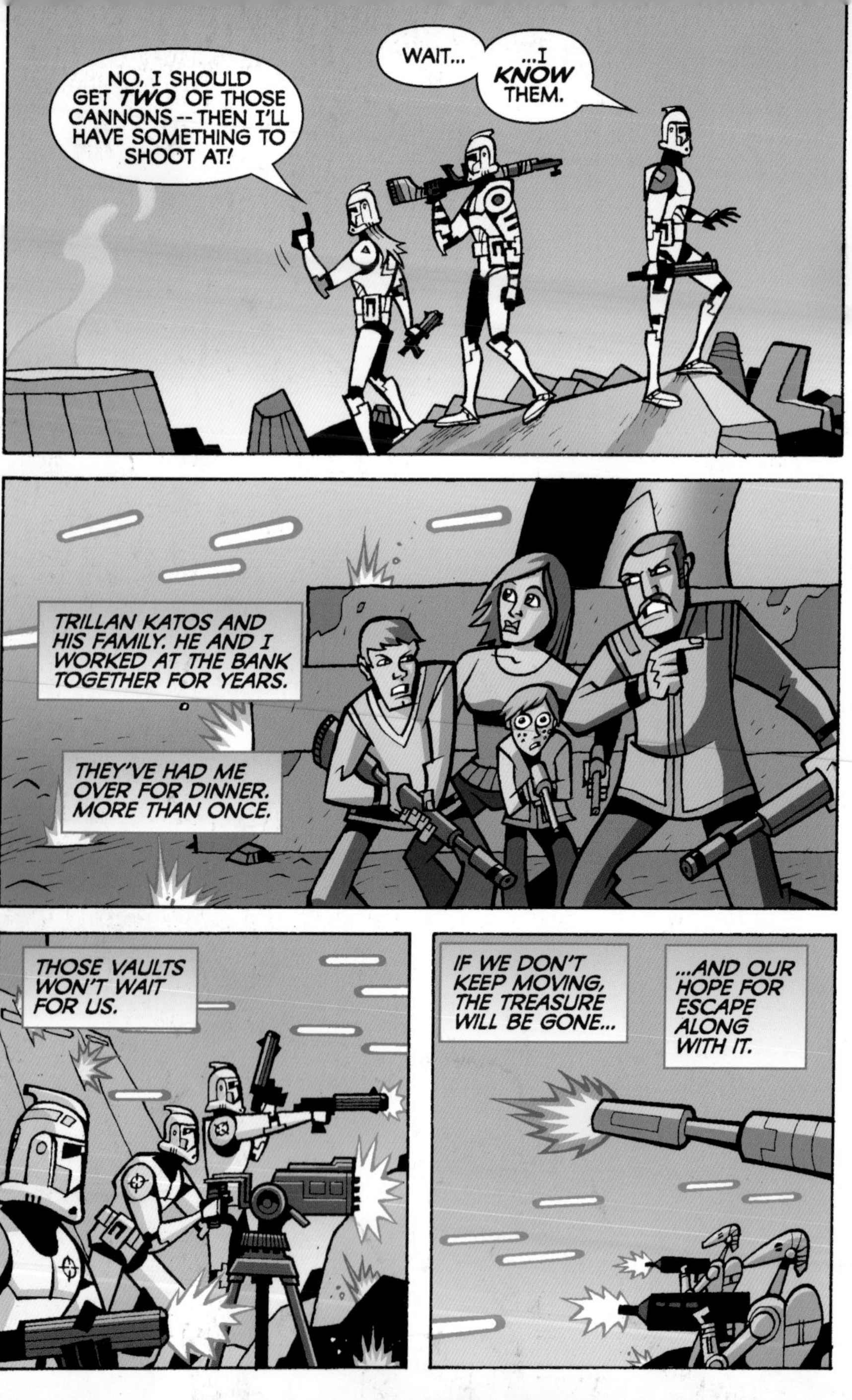
NO, I SHOULD GET TWO OF THOSE CANNONS -- THEN I'LL HAVE SOMETHING TO SHOOT AT!
WAIT...
...I KNOW THEM.
TRILLAN KATOS AND HIS FAMILY. HE AND I WORKED AT THE BANK TOGETHER FOR YEARS.
THEY'VE HAD ME OVER FOR DINNER. MORE THAN ONCE.
THOSE VAULTS WON'T WAIT FOR US.
IF WE DON'T KEEP MOVING, THE TREASURE WILL BE GONE...
...AND OUR HOPE FOR ESCAPE ALONG WITH IT.

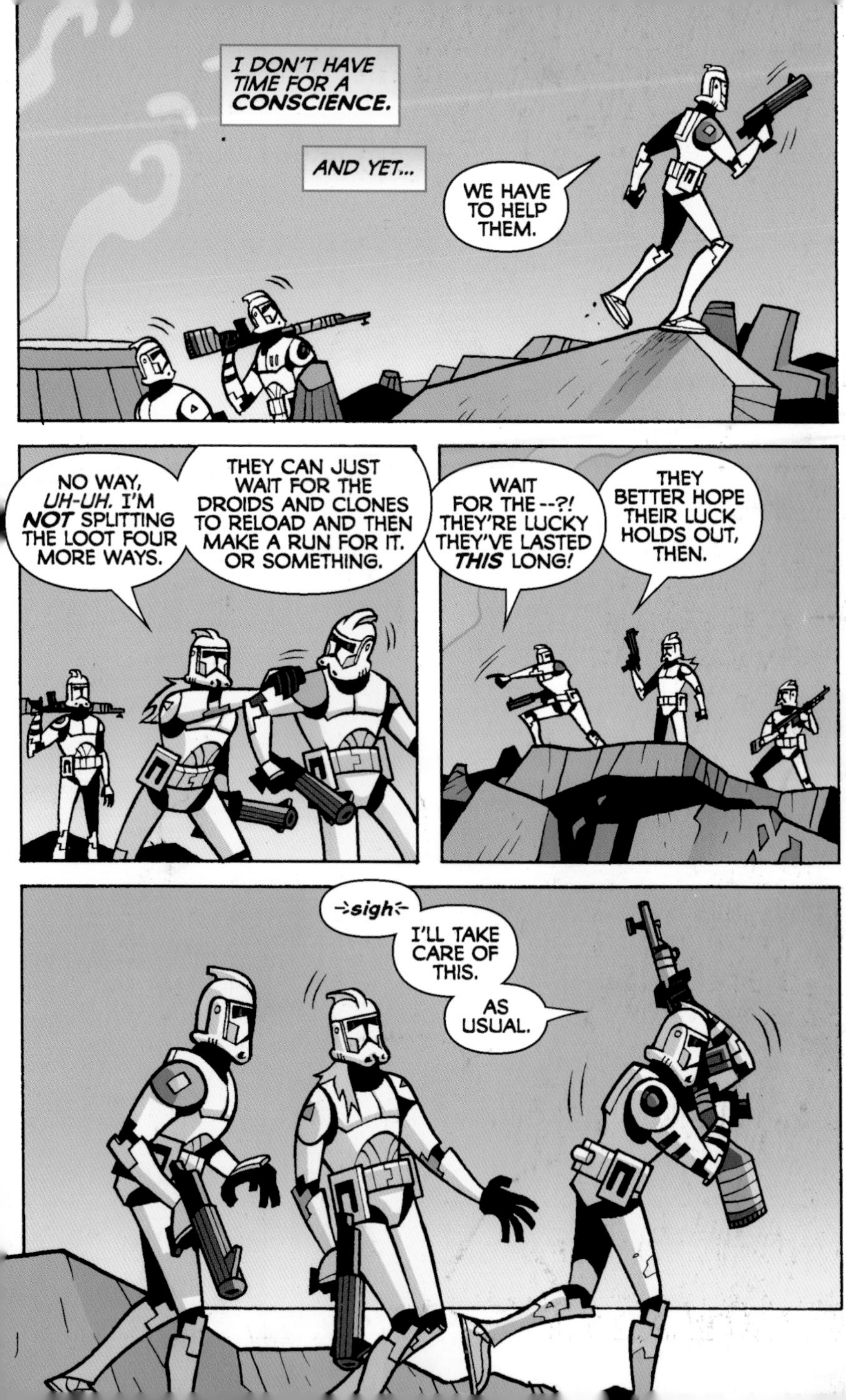

I DON'T HAVE TIME FOR A *CONSCIENCE.*
AND YET...
WE HAVE TO HELP THEM.
NO WAY, *UH-UH.* I'M ***NOT*** SPLITTING THE LOOT FOUR MORE WAYS.
THEY CAN JUST WAIT FOR THE DROIDS AND CLONES TO RELOAD AND THEN MAKE A RUN FOR IT. OR SOMETHING.
WAIT FOR THE--?! THEY'RE LUCKY THEY'VE LASTED ***THIS*** LONG!
THEY BETTER HOPE THEIR LUCK HOLDS OUT, THEN.
-sigh-
I'LL TAKE CARE OF THIS.
AS USUAL.

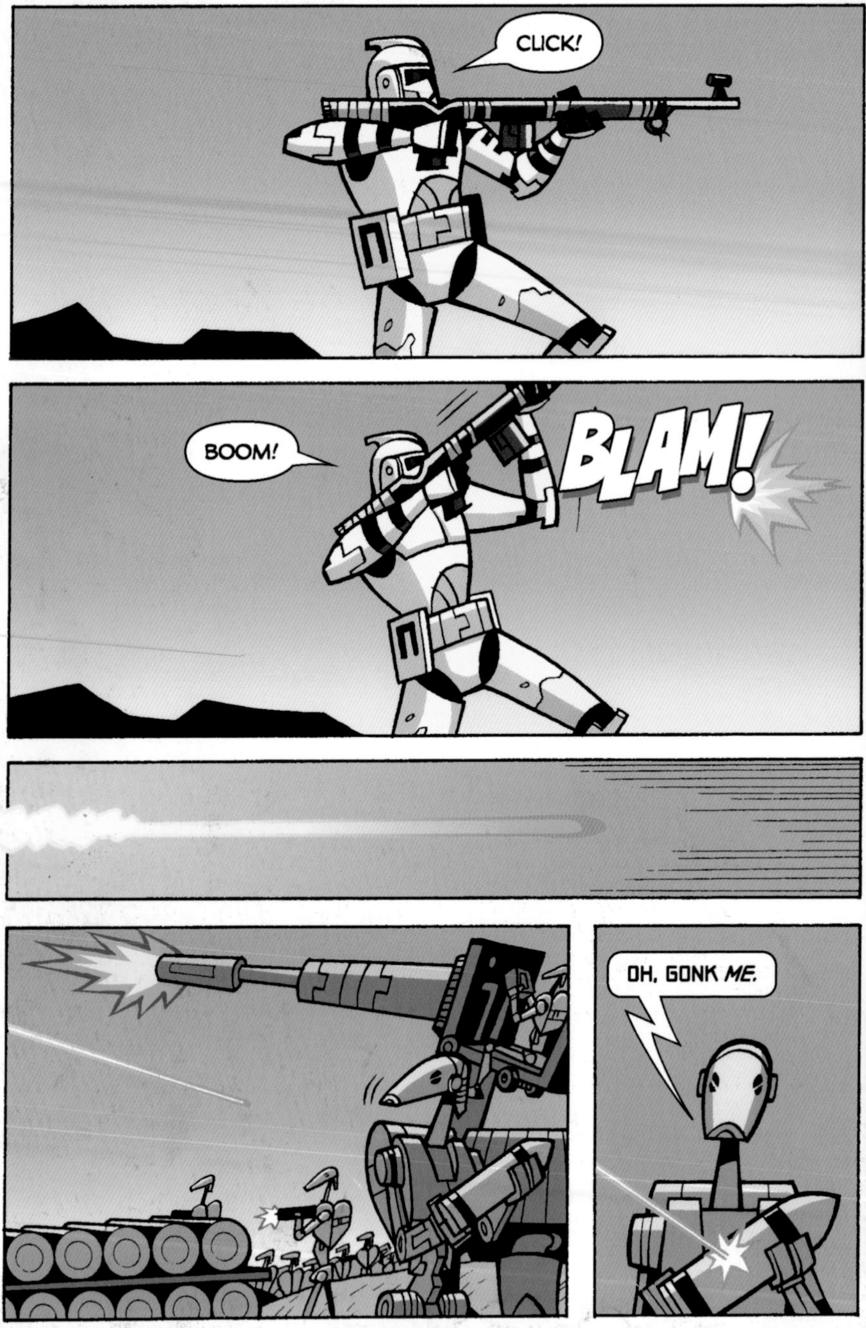
CLICK!
BOOM!
BLAM!
OH, GONK *ME.*

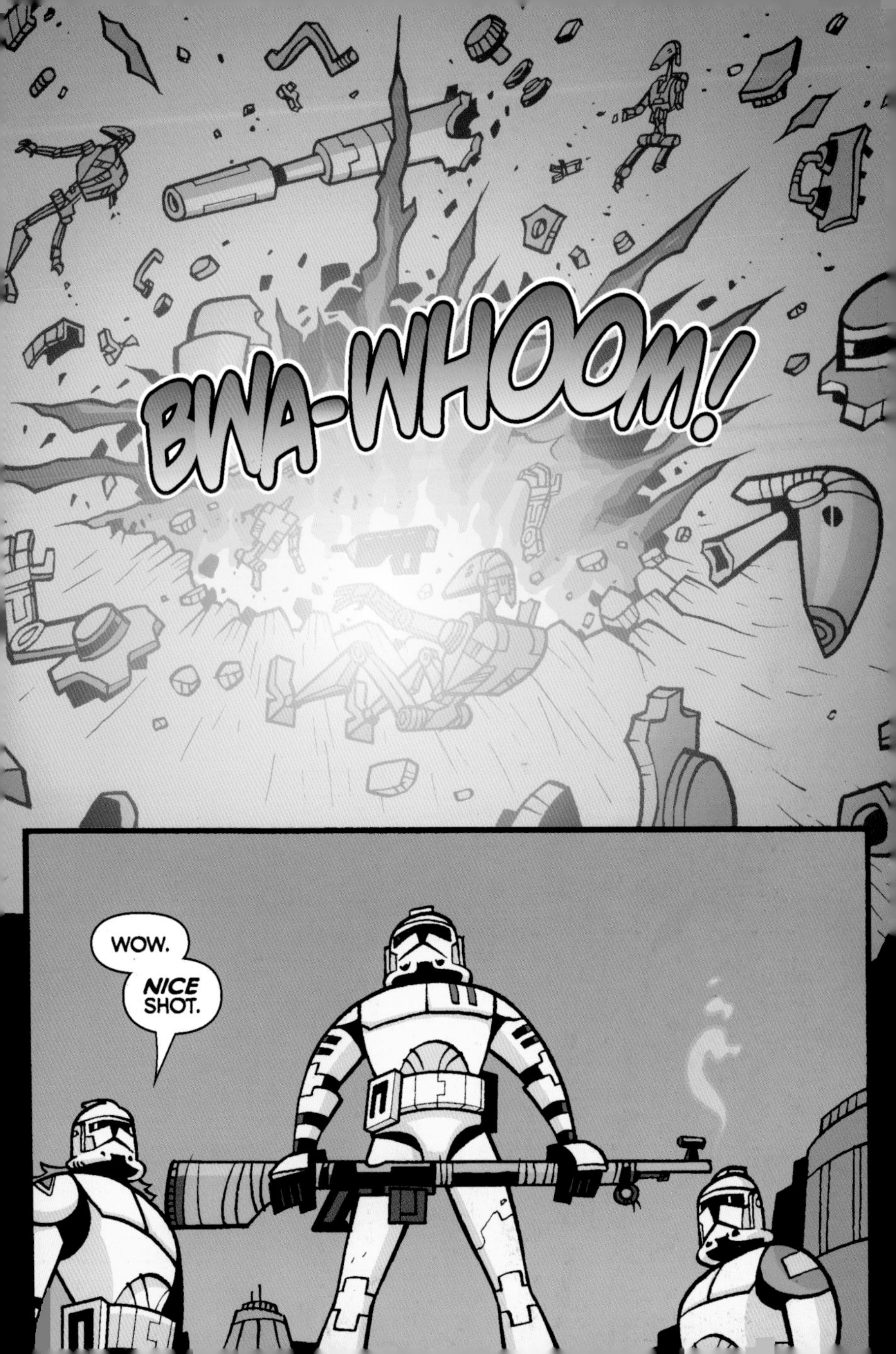
BWA-WHOOM!
WOW.
NICE SHOT.

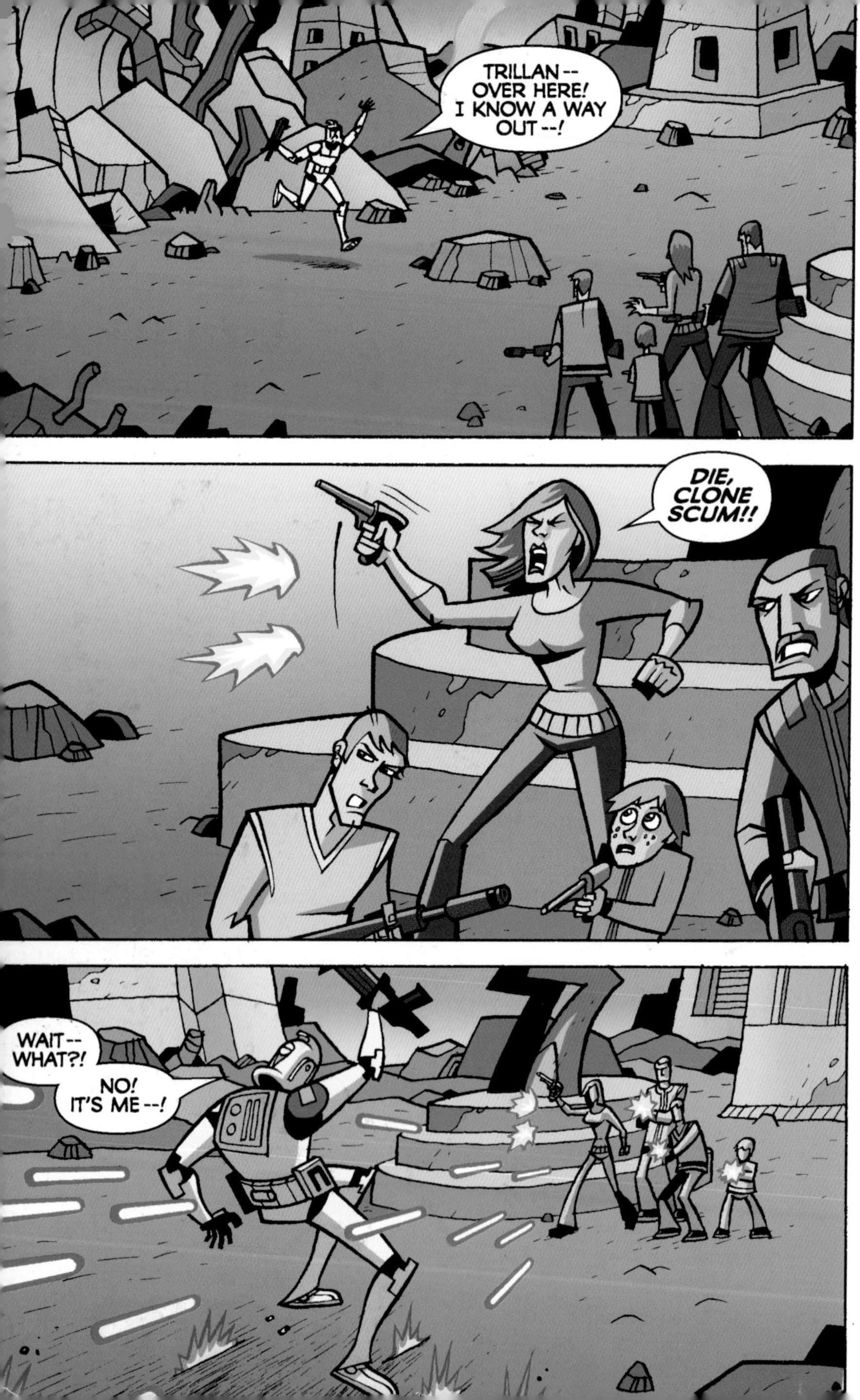
TRILLAN -- OVER HERE! I KNOW A WAY OUT --!
DIE, CLONE SCUM!!
WAIT -- WHAT?!
NO! IT'S ME --!

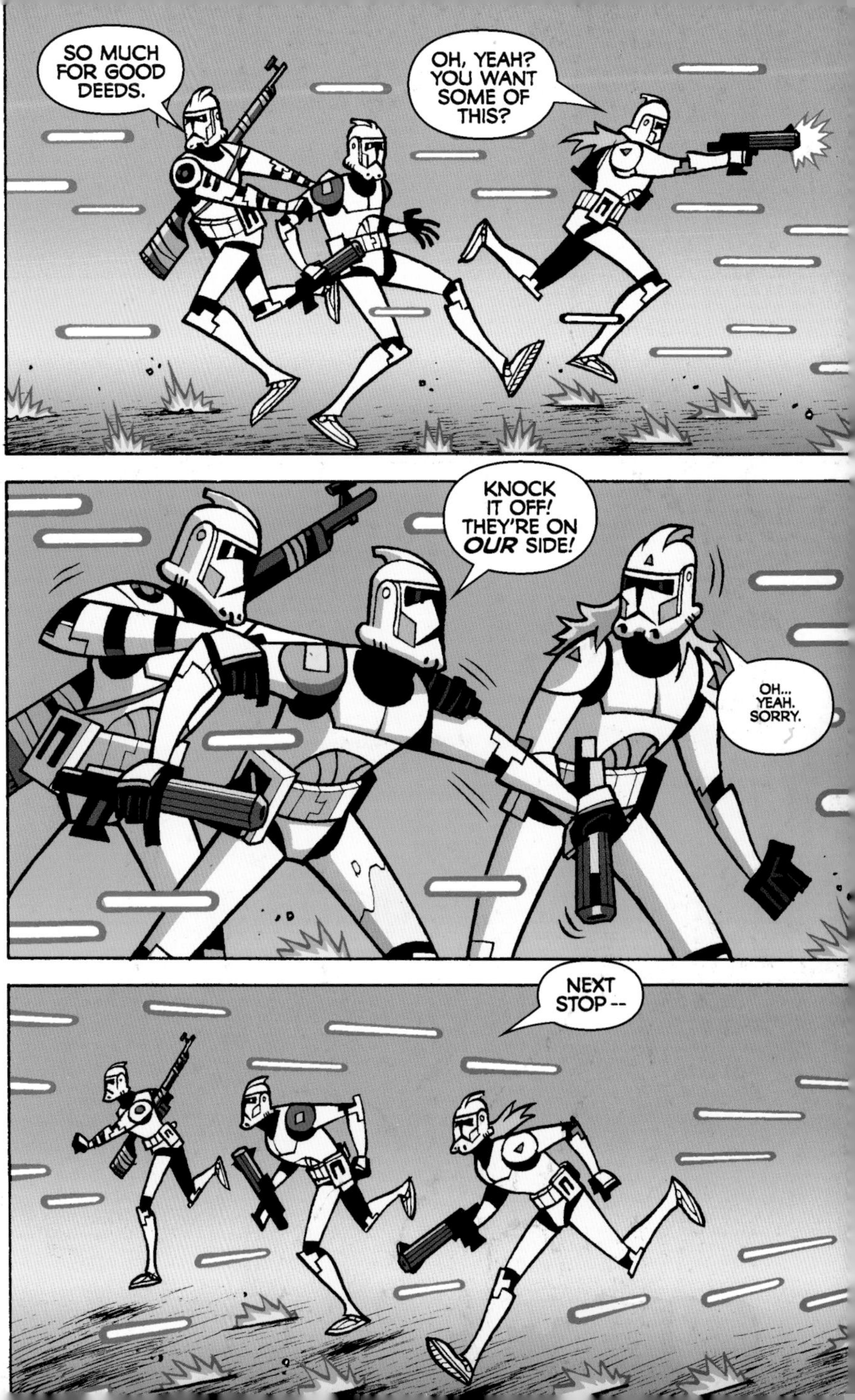
SO MUCH FOR GOOD DEEDS.
OH, YEAH? YOU WANT SOME OF THIS?
KNOCK IT OFF! THEY'RE ON *OUR* SIDE!
OH... YEAH. SORRY.
NEXT STOP --

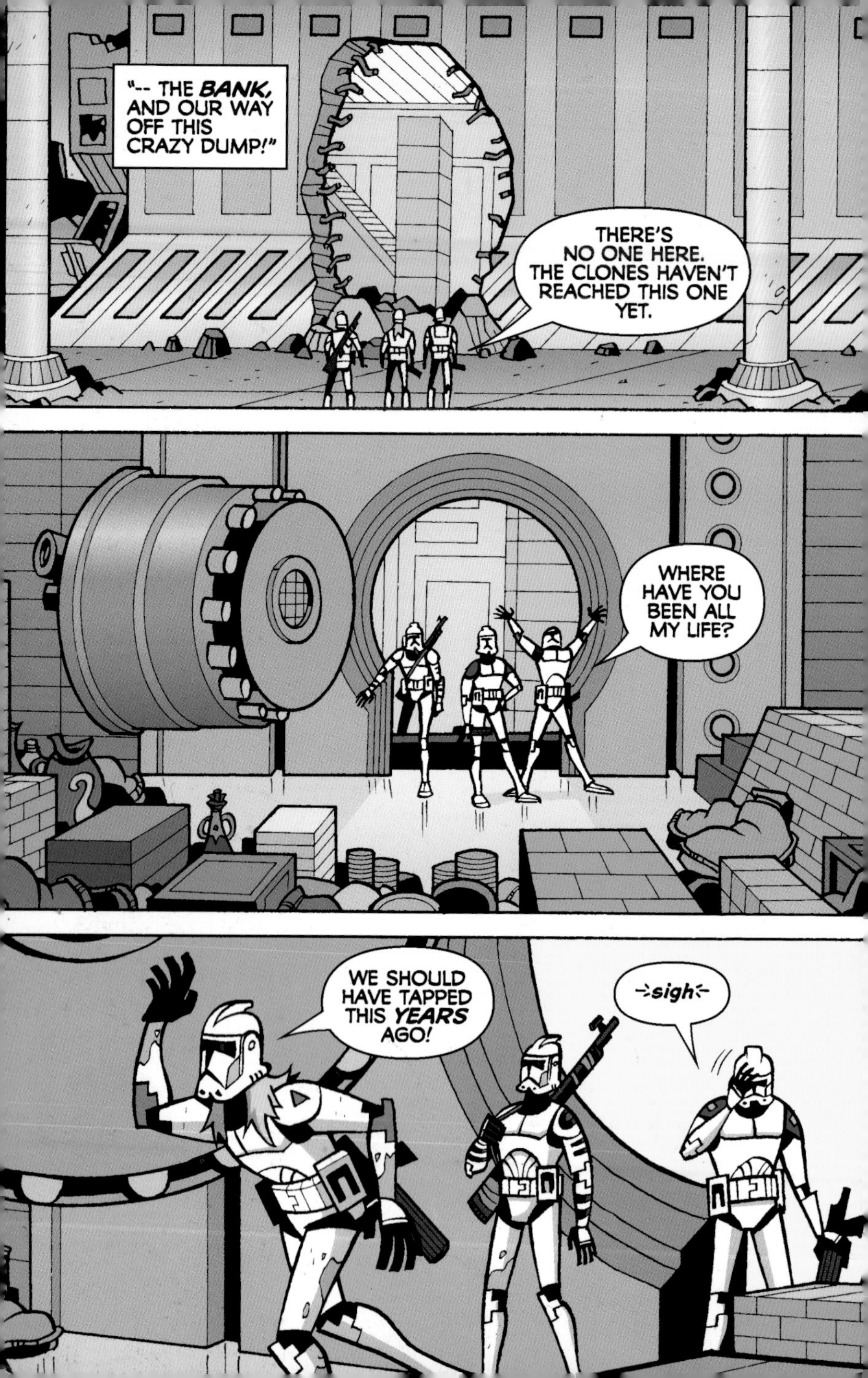
"-- THE *BANK,* AND OUR WAY OFF THIS CRAZY DUMP!"
THERE'S NO ONE HERE. THE CLONES HAVEN'T REACHED THIS ONE YET.
WHERE HAVE YOU BEEN ALL MY LIFE?
WE SHOULD HAVE TAPPED THIS *YEARS* AGO!
-sigh-

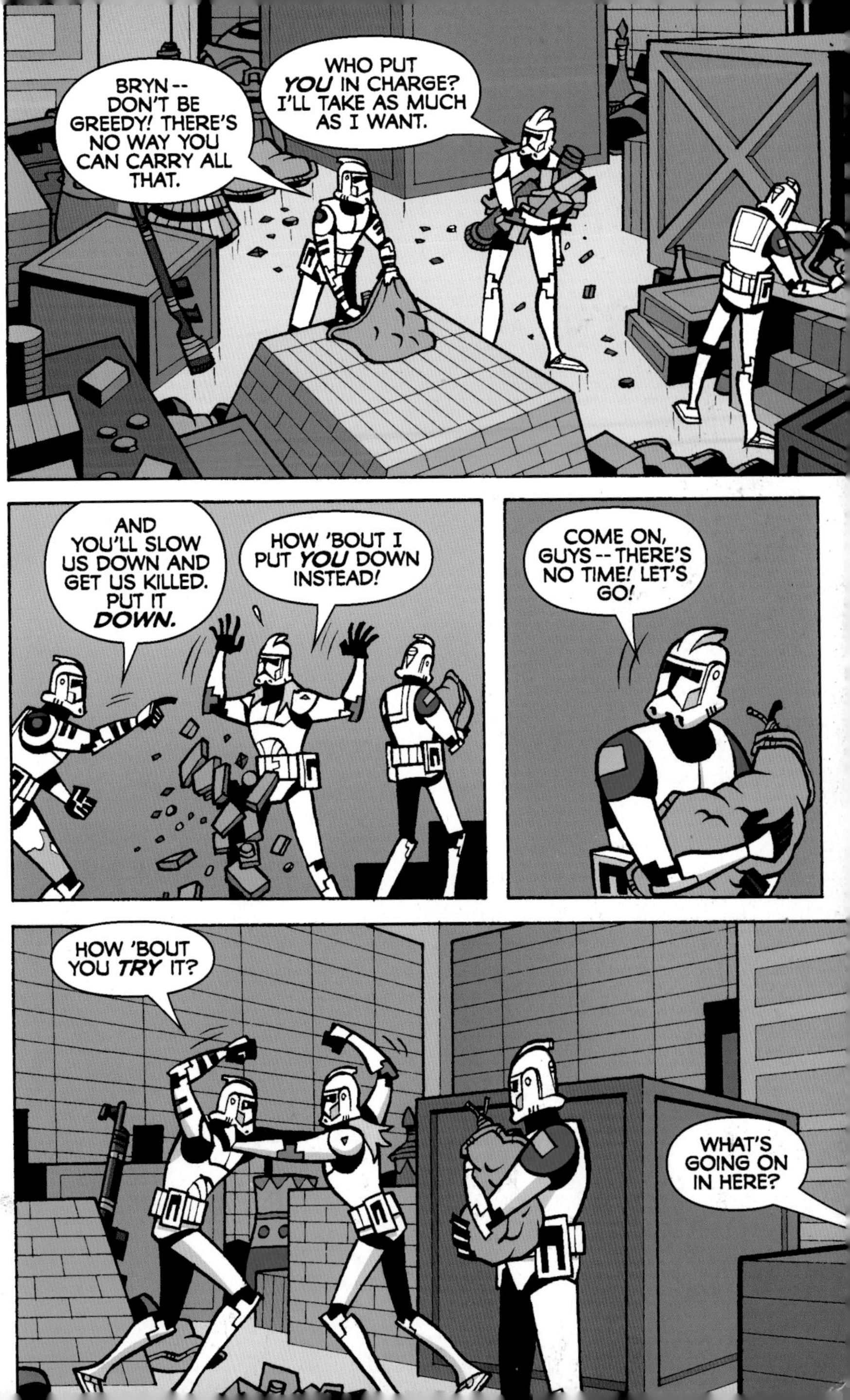
BRYN-- DON'T BE GREEDY! THERE'S NO WAY YOU CAN CARRY ALL THAT.
WHO PUT YOU IN CHARGE? I'LL TAKE AS MUCH AS I WANT.
AND YOU'LL SLOW US DOWN AND GET US KILLED. PUT IT DOWN.
HOW 'BOUT I PUT YOU DOWN INSTEAD!
COME ON, GUYS -- THERE'S NO TIME! LET'S GO!
HOW 'BOUT YOU TRY IT?
WHAT'S GOING ON IN HERE?

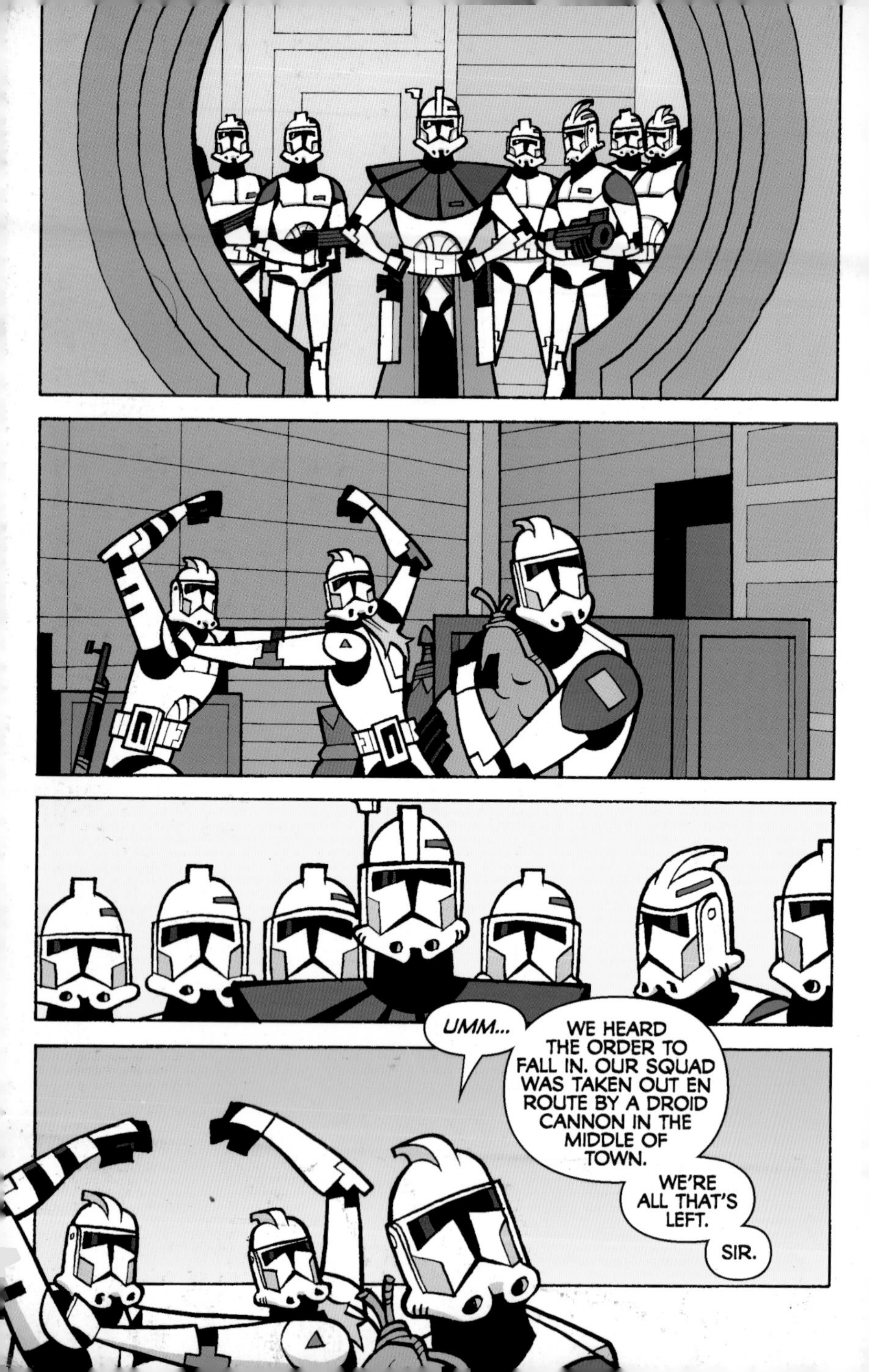
UMM...
WE HEARD THE ORDER TO FALL IN. OUR SQUAD WAS TAKEN OUT EN ROUTE BY A DROID CANNON IN THE MIDDLE OF TOWN.
WE'RE ALL THAT'S LEFT.
SIR.

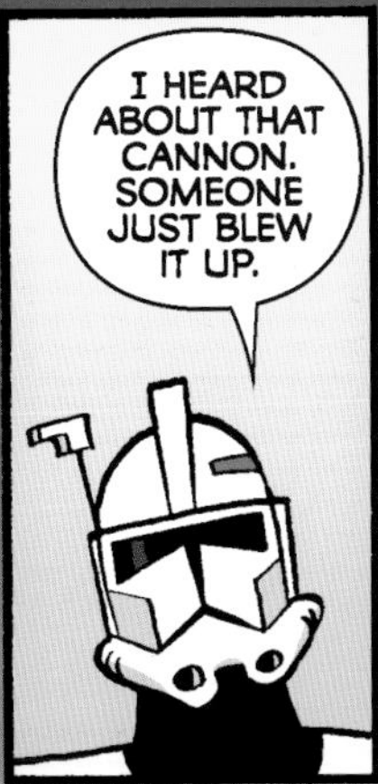
I HEARD ABOUT THAT CANNON. SOMEONE JUST BLEW IT UP.

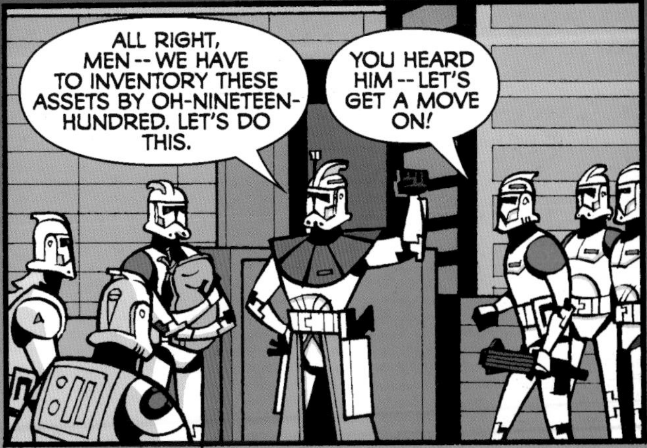
ALL RIGHT, MEN -- WE HAVE TO INVENTORY THESE ASSETS BY OH-NINETEEN-HUNDRED. LET'S DO THIS.
YOU HEARD HIM -- LET'S GET A MOVE ON!

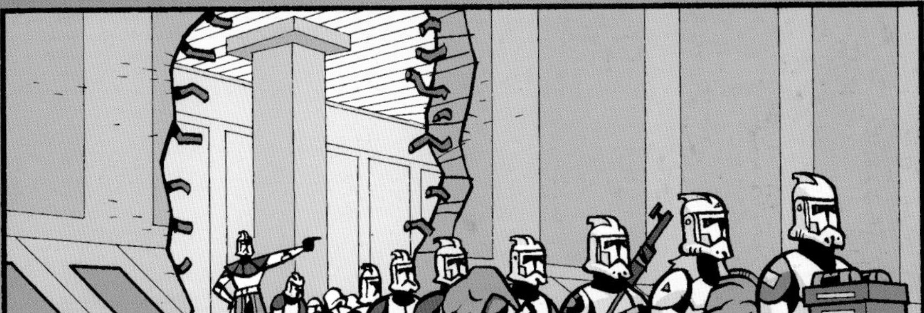

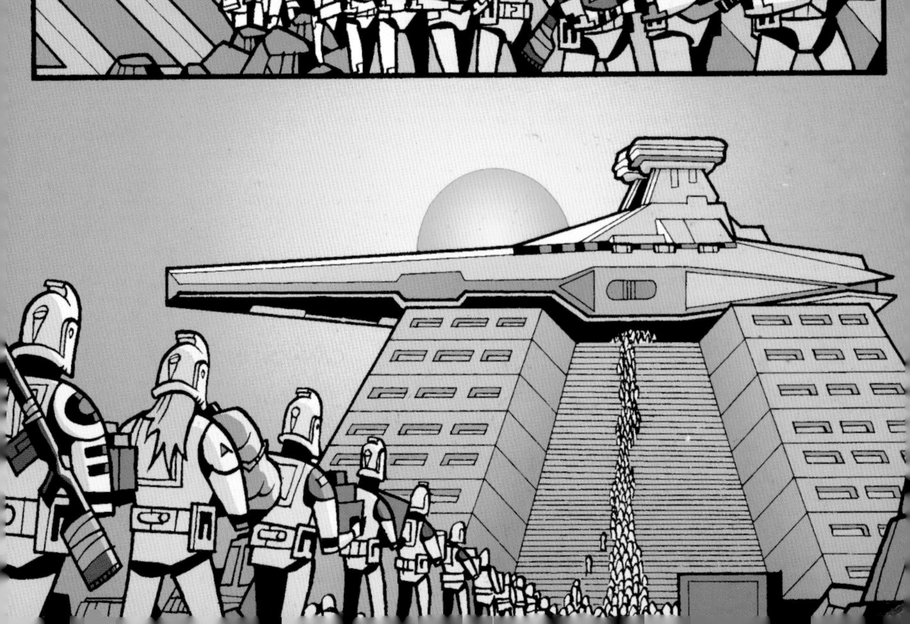

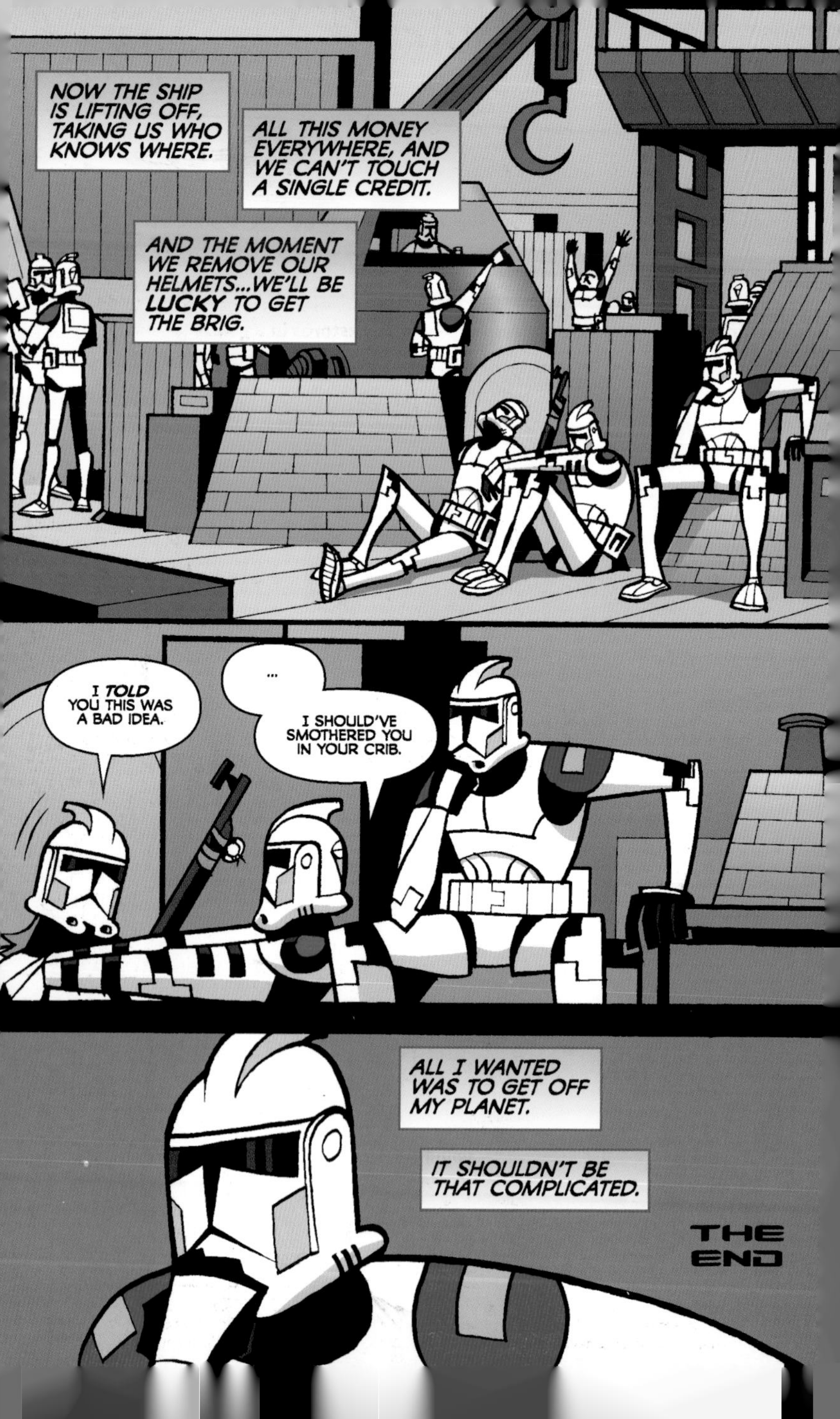
NOW THE SHIP IS LIFTING OFF, TAKING US WHO KNOWS WHERE.
ALL THIS MONEY EVERYWHERE, AND WE CAN'T TOUCH A SINGLE CREDIT.
AND THE MOMENT WE REMOVE OUR HELMETS...WE'LL BE LUCKY TO GET THE BRIG.
I TOLD YOU THIS WAS A BAD IDEA.
...
I SHOULD'VE SMOTHERED YOU IN YOUR CRIB.
ALL I WANTED WAS TO GET OFF MY PLANET.
IT SHOULDN'T BE THAT COMPLICATED.
THE END

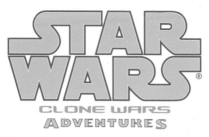

STAR WARS®
CLONE WARS ADVENTURES

Don't miss any of the action-packed adventures of your favorite STAR WARS® characters, available at comics shops and bookstores in a galaxy near you!

STAR WARS
CLONE WARS
ADVENTURES
THREE NEW STORIES! ALL-JEDI ACTION!

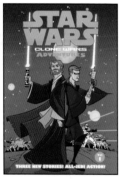

Volume 1
ISBN-10: 1-59307-243-0
ISBN-13: 978-1-59307-243-8

STAR WARS
CLONE WARS
ADVENTURES
THREE TALES OF HYPERKINETIC JEDI ACTION!

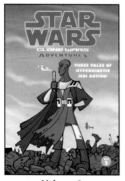

Volume 2
ISBN-10: 1-59307-271-6
ISBN-13: 978-1-59307-271-1

STAR WARS
CLONE WARS
ADVENTURES
FOUR TALES OF SINISTER SEPARATIST SCHEMING AND ROCKING REPUBLIC COMBAT!

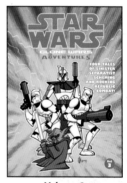

Volume 3
ISBN-10: 1-59307-307-0
ISBN-13: 978-1-59307-307-7

STAR WARS
CLONE WARS
ADVENTURES
FOUR RIVETING ADVENTURES IN ONE FANTASTIC VOLUME!

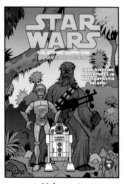

Volume 4
ISBN-10: 1-59307-402-6
ISBN-13: 978-1-59307-402-9

STAR WARS
CLONE WARS
ADVENTURES
FOUR AMAZING TALES OF HEROISM AND GALAXY-SHAKING ACTION!

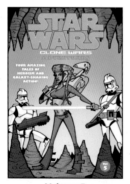

Volume 5
ISBN-10: 1-59307-483-2
ISBN-13: 978-1-59307-483-8

STAR WARS
CLONE WARS
ADVENTURES
FOUR TALES OF PLANETS IN PERIL AND JEDI IN JEOPARDY!

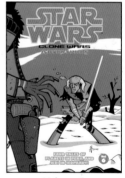

Volume 6
ISBN-10: 1-59307-567-7
ISBN-13: 978-1-59307-567-5

$6.95 each!

To find a comics shop in your area, call 1-888-266-4226
For more information or to order direct: • On the web: darkhorse.com • Phone: 1-800-862-0052. Mon.-Fri. 9 A.M. to 5 P.M. Pacific Time.
• E-mail: mailorder@darkhorse.com *Prices and availability subject to change without notice.

STAR WARS®
CLONE WARS

Experience all the excitement and drama of the
Clone Wars! Look for these trade paperbacks at
a comics shop or book store near you!

VOLUME 1: THE DEFENSE OF KAMINO
ISBN-10: 1-56971-962-4
ISBN-13: 978-1-56971-962-6
$14.95

VOLUME 2: VICTORIES AND SACRIFICES
ISBN-10: 1-56971-969-1
ISBN-13: 978-1-56971-969-5
$14.95

VOLUME 3: LAST STAND ON JABIIM
ISBN-10: 1-59307-006-3
ISBN-13: 978-1-59307-006-9
$14.95

VOLUME 4: LIGHT AND DARK
ISBN-10: 1-59307-195-7
ISBN-13: 978-1-59307-195-0
$16.95

VOLUME 5: THE BEST BLADES
ISBN-10: 1-59307-273-2
ISBN-13: 978-1-59307-273-5
$14.95

VOLUME 6: ON THE FIELDS OF BATTLE
ISBN-10: 1-59307-352-6
ISBN-13: 978-1-59307-352-7
$17.95

VOLUME 7: WHEN THEY WERE BROTHERS
ISBN-10: 1-59307-396-8
ISBN-13: 978-1-59307-396-1
$17.95

VOLUME 8: THE LAST SIEGE, THE FINAL TRUTH
ISBN-10: 1-59307-482-4
ISBN-13: 978-1-59307-482-1
$17.95

VOLUME 9: ENDGAME
ISBN-10: 1-59307-553-7
ISBN-13: 978-1-59307-553-8
$17.95

To find a comics shop in your area, call 1-888-266-4226
For more information or to order direct:
• On the web: darkhorse.com
• E-mail: mailorder@darkhorse.com
• Phone: 1-800-862-0052
Mon.-Fri. 9 A.M. to 5 P.M. Pacific Time
*Prices and availability subject to change
without notice. STAR WARS © 2006
Lucasfilm Ltd. & ™ (BL8018)

READY TO TRY SOME OTHER GREAT STAR WARS® TITLES?

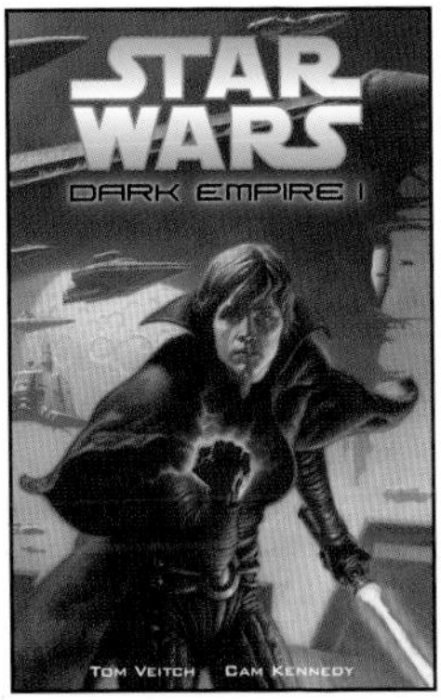
STAR WARS
DARK EMPIRE I
TOM VEITCH CAM KENNEDY

DARK EMPIRE

Join Luke, Leia, Han, and Chewie as they battle the Empire's latest super-weapons: the gigantic, planet-destroying World Devastators!

ISBN-10: 1-59307-039-X / ISBN-13: 978-1-59307-039-7

$16.95

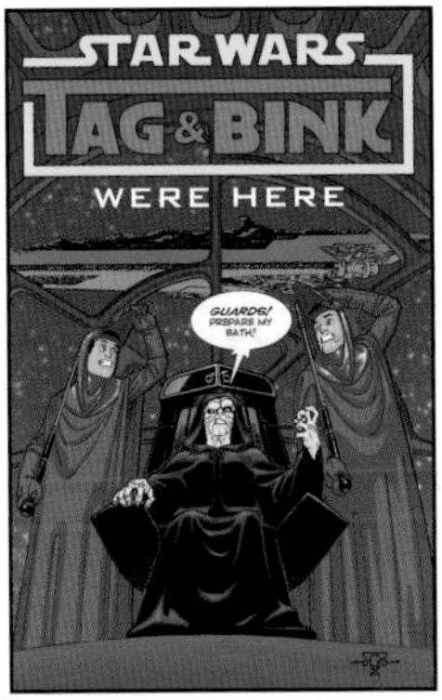
STAR WARS
TAG & BINK
WERE HERE
GUARDS! PREPARE MY BATH!

TAG AND BINK WERE HERE

Laugh yourself into orbit with the hilarious misadventures of a pair of hapless Rebel officers!

ISBN-10: 1-59307-641-X / ISBN-13: 978-1-59307-641-2

$14.95

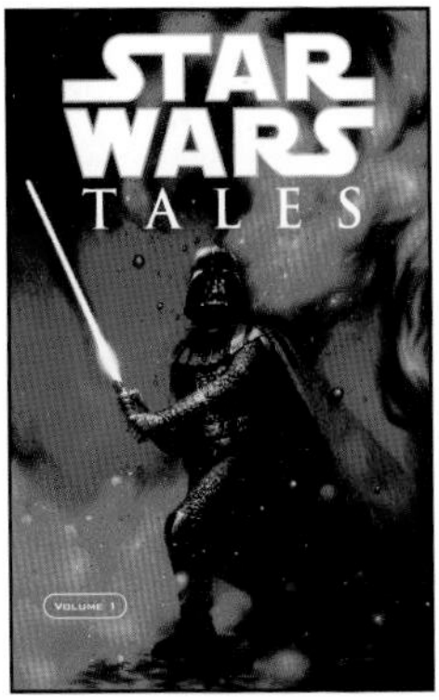
STAR WARS
TALES
VOLUME 1

TALES VOLUME 1

Read the first four issues of the quarterly anthology smash sensation that explores every corner of the *Star Wars* galaxy!

ISBN-10: 1-56971-619-6 / ISBN-13: 978-1-56971-619-9

$19.95

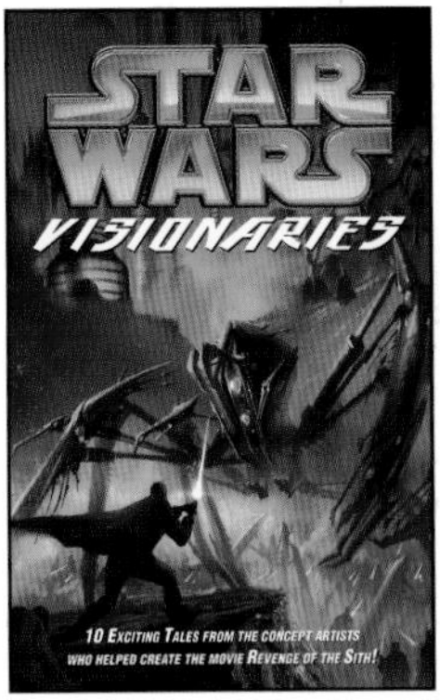
STAR WARS
VISIONARIES
10 EXCITING TALES FROM THE CONCEPT ARTISTS WHO HELPED CREATE THE MOVIE REVENGE OF THE SITH!

VISIONARIES

Ten exciting tales from the concept artists who helped create the movie *Revenge of the Sith*!

ISBN-10: 1-59307-311-9 / ISBN-13: 978-1-59307-311-4

$17.95

DARK HORSE BOOKS

AVAILABLE AT YOUR LOCAL COMICS SHOP OR BOOKSTORE!

To find a comics shop in your area, call 1-888-266-4226

For more information or to order direct visit darkhorse.com or call 1-800-862-0052 Mon.-Fri. 9 A.M. to 5 P.M. Pacific Time.

Prices and availability subject to change without notice.

DARK HORSE

darkhorse.com | DARK HORSE TWENTY YEARS

COMICS | BOOKS | PRODUCTS | REVIEWS | ZONES | NEWS | HELP | COMPANY | RESOURCES

VISIT THE

ZONE ON DARKHORSE.COM
TO EXPLORE GREAT FEATURES LIKE:

- Exclusive content from editors on upcoming projects!
- Download exclusive desktops!
- Online previews and animations!
- Message Boards!
- Up-to-date information on the latest releases!
- A complete *Star Wars* timeline!

Visit DARKHORSE.COM/STARWARS for more details!